I0814707

HOLLYWOOD *Stuntwoman*

DIANE PETERSON

Waterside Productions
Cardiff-by-the-Sea, California

Some names, locations, and identifying characteristics have been changed to protect the privacy of those depicted. Dialogue has been recreated from memory.

Cover design by Ken Fraser
www.impactbookdesigns.com

Printed in the United States of America
First Printing, 2022

ISBN-13: 978-1-957807-55-3 hardcover edition
ISBN-13: 978-1-957807-56-0 e-book edition

Waterside Productions
2055 Oxford Ave
Cardiff, CA 92007
www.waterside.com

This book is dedicated to my dear dad who taught me that I could do anything that I put my mind to. He always said, "You do your daddy proud." Thank you, Dad! I love you.

Contents

The True Story of a Woman Who Overcame Her Fears to Live Her Dream Life and Can Inspire You to Live Your Dream Life Too!

1

"How Did You Get into *That*?"

"Don't go near the edge, Diane, don't go near the edge!"

I could hear my mother's voice in my head as I stood on the tiny narrow ledge 120 feet above the ground. *Was I here because of rebellion? Or was I finally facing the fear of heights that had plagued me since childhood?* Every time I set foot on the upstairs outdoor porch with my brother, my mother would yell, "Don't go near the edge!"

Hearing my mother's warning made me want to go near the edge that much more, just to see what was on the other side. The temptation infused with full-blown fear riddling my miniature frame. Now thirty years later, the same infusion of fear pulsed through my entire body. Only this time it was my job to "go near the edge."

I can do this. I can do this.

Perched on the narrow ledge, twelve stories up, dressed in a nun's outfit. I was doubling Tracey Nelson, singer and actor Ricky Nelson's daughter, on the television series *Father Dowling Mysteries*. Below, the Denver, Colorado rush hour traffic came to a standstill as the horrified passengers observed a nun who seemed ready to plunge to her death. But my assignment was to inch my way along this minuscule ledge and enter the window to the room next door to help the person trapped inside!

The heart-stopping journey was twenty feet long, and midway across the ledge there was a three-foot gap that I would have to step over. Twelve stories below, the people on the street looked like ants.

I could hear my mother screaming, "Don't go near the edge!" as the show's hairdresser—safely rooted inside the building—fussed with my bangs and sprayed hairspray in my face.

I barked at her, "You stand on this ledge, and I'll spray hair spray in your face! No one is going to see my bangs!"

She made a hasty retreat.

Pummeled by terrifying what-ifs, I willed my mind to focus on a safe journey across the chasm. Having feared heights since my girlhood, I always must concentrate extra hard on overcoming the fear that lurks in the back of my mind. I did have a safety harness on under my nun's habit. If I fell, I would "only" fall twenty-five feet before jerking to a stop, hanging upside down against the side of the building, dangling like a rag doll. I would also probably die of fright by then, but it was still better than hitting the pavement! I asked God to keep me safe. I was in a Zen, trance-like state waiting for action.

Bobbing his head outside a nearby window, the show's assistant director asked, "How you doing?"

Nodding, with a smile, I gave a confident thumbs-up. The director was on the ground with a bullhorn. It seemed that I was waiting for an eternity for the cameramen to make last-minute adjustments. The age-old "don't go near the edge, don't go near the edge" pounded in my head. I'd overcome it before, and I'd do it this time. Though I knew better than to look down, I glanced and saw all the antlike figures staring up at me. Then my mind flooded with six words: "I'm going to do this perfectly."

Then the director screamed into his bullhorn, "Rolling, cameras, and action!"

My heart was racing as I slowly inched my way across the daunting ledge. I felt something tugging at my foot. *What the hell is that?* Careful to peer no further than my body, I shot a look down. My shoelace was untied! There was no way I could bend down and tie it. So, I kept inching my way along the ledge at a snail's pace. Nun's habit flying in the wind, clinging to the wall with my nails, I slowly extended my leg over the three-foot chasm. My foot barely reached the other side as I propelled myself over the abyss to avoid the peril below. My mouth was parched as I reached the window and finally climbed in. I heard "Cut!" and anxiously awaited the director's voice saying, "It's a print. We're moving on."

But that's not what he said.

"Diane," he coached, "that was good but let's do it again, a little faster this time."

"No problem," I replied instinctively, tying my shoelace, and preparing to go again. This time I decided to give them a little bang for their buck! Having traversed the ledge successfully once, I was feeling more confident, so I maneuvered an intentional trip when crossing the abyss. As I awkwardly fell onto one knee, I heard the collective gasp from those below. Slowly and carefully,

I picked myself up and gingerly climbed into the window.

The director yelled, "Cut, that's a print, we are moving on. That was great! You're amazing, Diane."

It wasn't the first time I had to face my fear of heights, and it wouldn't be my last.

One of my earliest memories was riding Smokey, a little black pony with a white-striped nose, at the pony track in New Jersey. I was about three years old. While the ponies were being walked around the track, all the other little kids were crying and hanging onto their mommies and daddies. As soon as I was put on the back of Smokey, I wanted to be set free. I made the pony run around the track and rear up much to the amazement of my father, and the horror of my mother. Riding, and riding *fast*, felt natural, and soon I was riding every Saturday morning. I quickly began riding in parades. My dad ran alongside me as I rode Smokey down the boulevard in my hometown, Elmwood Park, New Jersey. I waved to the crowds with a smile, ear to ear, dressed in a cowgirl outfit with cute little red boots. At home, I took on the play name of "Sheriff Randal," and my days were filled with anticipation of riding the range with my pal Smokey.

Around the same time, my mother enrolled me in ballet classes with a cranky old woman teacher named Lila Crabtree. Miss Crabtree had rolls of fat stuffed into a tight black leotard. She would force my legs in uncomfortable positions and shout French words in my face. She wore bright-red lipstick that was smeared all over her face, her hair was messy, and she smelled like a dirty ashtray. I was completely bored with the repetitions, and I hated the tutus that I was coerced into wearing. I soon refused to go to class. But my mother laid down the law: no ballet class, no pony rides. Ugh! What a sacrifice! Could I bear the weekly hour of torture? I had to because I loved that pony. When

I was four years old, I was preparing to dance in my first recital. I got to wear a pretty little butterfly costume. I liked that. On the night of the big show, I was not feeling well. My mom, dad, and Miss. Crabtree taught me a life lesson that I never forgot: "The show must go on!" Yes, the show must go on. I donned my little wings and kicked up my legs. My daddy brought me flowers, and I felt like a real ballerina. The next day I came down with the measles.

When I was about six years old, I got my first little pink bicycle with long white streamers flying off the handlebars. I didn't like the training wheels in back at all, and I whined and begged my daddy to take them off. Finally, one day he said I was ready to ride solo. My daddy ran behind the bike. I pedaled like a mad-woman and soon I was flying down a huge hill. I turned and looked back at my daddy laughing, and I was on my own way! I rode every day after school. I looked for the biggest hill, trying to go faster and faster, finding jumps to soar over, wind in my long blond hair. I never got tired of exploring and pedaling my little pink bike around town.

Elmwood Park, New Jersey, was a wonderful place to grow up and develop my need for speed. It was a tough town too, not far from the George Washington Bridge and New York City. You needed to gain your street smarts at an early age. One day, a fat little girl with freckles and glasses tried to steal my bike. I punched her in the face and broke her glasses. My daddy had always told me to get the first punch in. He forgot to tell me to never hit a kid with glasses on!

That event was the beginning of my fight scenes!

The Ringling Bros. and Barnum & Bailey Circus at Madison Square Garden changed my life when I was about seven years old. My parents got front row seats for my brother John and me. I was mesmerized by the tightrope walker.

"Mommie, that's what I want to be when I grow up," I proudly exclaimed.

"No, no, you don't, honey," my mom insisted. "You'd live like a gypsy in tents all your life." Ha! Sounded good to me!

A few days later while Mom was cooking in the kitchen, I found some rope in the garage. I talked my brother John into tying the rope around two wing chairs in the living room. I was about to make my debut as the tightrope walker when my mom came around the corner and screamed, "Stop it, Diane, you are going to fall and kill yourself!" My dreams of taking my first tightrope walk were shattered. But the Ringling Bros. and Barnum & Bailey had planted the seed. It would be twenty years later that I stepped onto my first real tightrope.

We moved to our new, beautiful ranch house on North Street. We had woods in our backyard and my dad put a thick rope around a mighty branch in a huge tree. The rope had an enormous knot at the bottom, and my brother and I would take turns climbing up the six-foot ladder, jumping off, and sailing through the air. We would pile leaves into a haystack-sized catcher and would jump off the rope and fall into the mounds of colorful autumn leaves.

When it snowed, my dad would shovel the snow into a bank next to the roof of our house. We would climb onto the roof and jump off. The first time we jumped, we sailed past the window where my mom was feverishly typing bills for my father's trucking company. She nearly had a heart attack. I think my dad might have gotten into some big trouble over setting that stunt up!

One hot, humid summer day in Jersey when I was seven, my brother and I were helping my dad pick up branches and small debris from our large, woodsy backyard. This day we had an incentive. My dad said when we filled his little 1947 green Dodge panel truck to the brim with branches, we would go to the dump and he would teach us how to drive. Oh, this was the day I was waiting for. We worked like beavers filling the truck with dead limbs and unwanted neighbors' trash that blew into our backyard paradise. We were then on our way to the DPW, the Department of Public Works that would serve in my imagination as my first racetrack.

"I'm going first," I squealed to my older brother.

I was filled with eager anticipation of getting behind the wheel. My dad opened the enormous rusty gates and we slowly drove into this land of junk piles. There was a huge pile of discarded washing machines, refrigerators, and car parts with a circular road going around it. We quickly emptied our load of tree waste in the proper area, and bingo! It was time to drive!

"Me first!"

I ran around the truck and climbed into the well-worn leather seat. The steering wheel was giant, and my feet could barely reach the pedals. My dad propped some pillows behind me and showed me the shift control, which was on the steering column.

"OK, push the clutch in with your left foot, slide the shift handle upward into gear, and slowly let go," explained my dad.

Bam! I popped the clutch and launched us on our way. I immediately stomped on the gas with my right foot, hung onto the wheel, and turned it like a whirling dervish around the huge mound of trash. That was it! I was born to drive! I was loving every second of my newfound talent. My brother demanded his turn, and I reluctantly gave up the wheel.

That was it . . . my introduction to being behind the wheel. I was just a little seven-year-old girl, but I knew that I loved to drive and go fast. Little did I know what would develop from this spark of joy I felt in my soul. My dad let me drive as much as possible because he saw how much I loved it. Dirt roads and parking lots became my training ground. My dad owned a trucking company called Plaza Trucking, and he loved what he did! There was not a day that he complained about going to work. He was his own boss and did things his way.

While my dad was equipping me for adventure, my mom was entering me in lots of little kid beauty pageants. I had to have my hair curled and wear silly little dresses. It was good practice, I suppose, to help me get rid of any anxiety of being in front of crowds or being judged. I was constantly being judged in pageants, horse shows, and in school. I was fierce about wanting to win, and it took a long time for me to be able to handle losing or rejection. I still don't like it. Who would? But I learned to handle those tough times and rejection with ease and grace.

I lived life as a daring, adventurous journey as I learned to overcome my fears and enjoy the thrill of trying new challenges. True to who he was, Dad instilled and nurtured the daring in me. And true to who she was, my mom peppered my adventures with warnings of caution. Both would one day prove very useful!

I think it's fair to say that when I was young, few—if any—little girls were dreaming of growing up to perform stunts for cameras! But today I can recognize the clues pointing toward the woman I would one day become. The satisfaction I got from riding the pony in the parade and driving the little truck around in the dump, as well as the rush of adrenaline I got when taking calculated risks that most would avoid, were essential parts of who I was made to be. And every time I honored those, and conquered my fears, I would be one step closer to the work and purpose for which I was made.

When you think back to your earliest days, can you remember what you were doing when you felt unbridled joy? Do you remember what you could have done for hours and felt like no time had passed at all? While many dismiss those early experience as "child's play," they may provide critical clues to the unique purpose for which you were made. Maybe you stayed up late scribbling stories in a journal about the racecar driver you would become. Or you may have dreamed about being an astronaut! Or maybe you found a special satisfaction when you were climbing mountains in the hills behind your house. When you pause to notice what gave you joy during childhood—and today!—you'll have valuable data to discover your unique purpose and to make a plan to follow your dream. Whatever you dream you can be!

2

Jumping, Racing, and Looking Pretty

"You just got the wind knocked out of you, honey."

I'd been riding a large headstrong Appaloosa pony named Dynamite, white with brown spots decorating his hindquarters, when he got spooked right before a jump. At the last second, Dynamite slammed on the brakes just inches in front of the fence I'd expected us both to clear. Because I'd moved into my jumping position, forward in the saddle, I sailed over the fence and landed flat on my back.

Stunned, wind knocked out of me, and wheezing for breath, I opened my eyes to see my father leaning over me.

"You'll be okay. Let's walk around slowly," he encouraged me.

Turning to one of the stable hands who'd rushed over, he calmly instructed, "Get her some water, please."

Helping me to my feet, he stayed at my side as we began to walk together in a small circle and return to Dynamite's side.

When I began to feel like myself again, I announced, "Dad, I'm ready. Let's go home."

Pausing and turning to look me in the eye, my dad gently coached, "Baby, you need to get right back on Dynamite and try that jump again."

My hand stroked Dynamite on the muzzle as I listened to his words.

My dad continued, "If you don't, you'll never want to ride horses for the rest of your life. You need to conquer your fear immediately and go for it."

Although it was the last thing I wanted to do, I trusted my dad. Mounting up, I slipped my feet into the stirrups. Cantering around the dusty ring, I willed myself to be brave as we picked up speed and approached the fence. As if he was a different horse, Dynamite and I sailed over the fence.

After a few more months, I graduated to higher jumps and a bigger horse named Tiny Tim. My riding instructor, Jerry Johnson, was the only person riding Timmy. One day, I was granted permission to climb on his back. I longed to ride this handsome bay gelding with the long black mane and tail. He pranced like a Lipizzaner and jumped fences like a cat. I quickly learned that I had to "stay awake" on his back—no daydreaming while riding this powerful horse. Timmy and I got along great. I was light as a feather, and he liked that compared to the weight of Jerry. I could feel his sensitive mouth through my grip on the reins. We began jumping fences that were higher and higher. He liked to rear up and charge the fence. I gripped the saddle with my knees and held him back with his head up high until we sailed through the air over the fence. We were one in motion and spirit, and I loved this horse.

When I was about twelve years old, we began entering horse shows in the Junior Jumper Class and took the circuit by storm. I was beating all the top riders and horses in Bergen County and New York State. My collection of blue ribbons, championship ribbons, and sterling silver trophies started to fill my bedroom. Then one day on the ride home from the stable, my dad told me that Warren Hauser, Tiny Tim's owner, had lost the lease on the barn and had to sell all the horses. I was devastated. I loved that horse more than I loved life. I cried and cried uncontrollably. My dad said we would be going to the stable on the next Saturday to say goodbye to Timmy. I dreaded the idea of saying goodbye to the best horse I had ever ridden. I cried myself to sleep every night. Saturday morning arrived way too soon. My dad and I drove to the stable not saying a word to each other. It was a long, sad journey. When we arrived at the parking lot, I reluctantly shuffled to the stable entrance holding my dad's hand, fighting back the tears. As we stepped inside, Timmy put his head outside the stall, and he had a giant green bow tied around his neck. I looked at my dad and he said, "Happy birthday, baby." I could not believe it! It was the greatest present any little girl could ever have. Timmy was mine, all mine. I hugged my dad so hard, thanking him, and with tears running down my face I flew to the stall door and grabbed Timmy and just kept kissing him. I still well up with tears whenever I think of the special gift my parents gave me that day.

During high school, I actually had a mini stunt job that would follow me for several years. I was the "Bongo" girl. Yes, for Bongo Boards! The Bongo Board was very much like a circus performer's teeter-totter. There was a wooden platform that I had to balance on over a round wooden cylinder. I won a ski queen contest at Stoney Point, New York. One of the producers noticed my athletic ability and suggested that I go to New York City and meet Merrill and Flo Decker, the terrific couple who ran the Bongo Board Company. My dad drove me to Sutton Place South, where they lived, and we instantly hit it off. I hopped on the Bongo Board, and I was a natural. They hired me to do my first of many ski trade shows in the New York City Coliseum. I wore a hot, tight ski outfit and a large crowd of mostly young males gathered around to cheer me on. The Deckers paid me very well and the sales of Bongo Boards soared. They even had milk chocolate bars made with my picture on the Bongo Board. I soon began balancing on it one way and jumping into the air and turning 180 degrees and landing on the board facing backward. The crowd would go wild, and I loved every minute of it. The Deckers were wonderful people and they introduced me to positive thinking with the book *Think and Grow Rich* by Napoleon Hill. The granddaddy of motivational books, written in 1937, drew on the stories of successful business moguls like Andrew Carnegie, Henry Ford, and Thomas Edison. Hill's "Law of Success" philosophy was built on the power of positive thinking. The Deckers had a profound influence on my life. The power of positive thinking rests deep within my soul.

At sixteen, I learned to ride my brother's Triumph Bonneville motorcycle. It was so hard to kick-start that when I took it out for a spin, I had to make sure I stopped where there were some guys so I could ask them to jump-start it for me. One day, Warren Flagler, an amazing New York City photographer, asked if he could photograph me on the motorcycle. My brother said I could take the bike, and off I went to the photo shoot. The picture wound up on my first album cover, *Rock Explosion*. Warren also photographed Tiny Tim in a full rear with me on his bare back! My favorite shot that Warren did was of me leaping through the air in a bikini. That shot wound up on the cover of a magazine! He really knew how to capture me in action.

When I was sixteen and a half, it was time to get my first car. The driving age was seventeen in New Jersey. What a joke—I already had ten years' experience. In fact, I won the parallel parking contest in high school hands down. I wanted a Corvette or a Jaguar, and I begged my dad, assuring him I'd saved $350 toward the down payment from my job in the local 5 and 10 cent store as a short-order cook.

My dad laughed and said, "Let's go look."

We looked at both cars, and my dad said he thought it was better to buy an American car, so we ordered my very first Corvette! Corvette Bronze, a burnt orange, was the color I picked. I could hardly wait for its arrival. There was a steel strike, which caused a delay, and then my car was finally delivered. I was so thrilled, proud, and thankful! This would be the first of my three Corvettes. I owned them for a total of forty-two years!

My brother had a Shelby GT350 and decided that he wanted to try racing in quarter-mile drag races. It looked like fun to me, too. So, we took white shoe polish and wrote Big Bro on his Shelby and Lil Sis on my Corvette and headed to English Town Raceway. My Corvette was a four speed with a 350-horsepower engine and was fast—very fast.

On the way there, my dad said, "Whatever you do, don't beat him, it will cost me money! Your brother will want me to have his engine blueprinted to make it go faster!"

Ha! I began to understand the male ego in some small way. His car was actually faster than mine. He had 428 horsepower, and the only way I could beat him was if he missed a shift. I felt the need for speed as we waited on the grid for the Christmas tree lights to blink down. My heart pumped furiously, and my focus was only on winning. Green light and I floored the Vette and peeled off the tarmac, getting just the right jump out of the gate.

I heard John's engine roaring next to me. Pedal to the metal, I hugged the wheel and flew down the runway. My brother must have missed a shift because I was ahead of him. I remembered my dad's words, eased up a bit, and he won by a nose. For the next few years, John and I amassed a bunch of trophies, and the weekends were always exciting. My timing proved to be excellent. Years later, I would win the Drag Race Championship in 2006 at a Corvette Meet in Georgia. All these driving skills led to my first "car stunt job" in New York City years later.

One weekend we would go to the horse show, and the next weekend we would go to the drag races. My dad enjoyed the excitement of watching his kids have fun as much as we enjoyed the action. Unfortunately, my mother got stuck staying home to take care of my bedridden grandmother most weekends. She missed out on a lot of fun.

I broke my collarbone one night by stupidly horsing around with the kids at the local park. We were playing leapfrog. As I leaped over one guy, he decided to crouch down. I sailed over his back and landed on my shoulder. The orthopedic doctor put a rather strong cast around my shoulders to stabilize the collarbone. It was the same collarbone that was broken during my delivery into the world. I had a modeling job photo shoot in two weeks, and I really wanted to do it. It was for a nail polish company. I begged my dad to crack open the cast so I could slide out for the job. He got a pair of hedge clippers and mangled the side of the cast under my arm. I was free. He drove me to the job, and I posed for the shoot. I slipped back into the cast and my dad taped it shut. When we went back to the doctor for the follow up visit, he was furious. My dad was one in a million!

When I attended the University of Miami in Coral Gables, Florida, I decided to sign up with a local modeling agency to make a few extra bucks. I got a call from my new agent, and she asked if I could ride a horse bareback. I promptly replied that I could gallop a horse bareback, no problem. So, off I went to the interview in my form-fitting blue jeans, bright-red tank top, and well-worn cowboy boots. The interview just happened to be at a horse ranch. Twenty young blonds anxiously waited to mount the huge black horse minus a saddle. I could hardly wait to get my turn. I laughed on the inside as I saw my competition timidly climbing on the back of the striking steed and then sit frozen in fear. Excitement rose up in me as they called my name. I smiled brightly, smoothly mounted the gorgeous horse, and took off in a fast gallop. My long blond hair was flying in the wind as I giggled and laughed all the way to the end of the dusty trail and back. I nailed that one! The following week we filmed the commercial for a land development company on the beach at daybreak. I was in all my glory galloping the big, beautiful black horse at sunrise on the pristine beach and getting paid handsomely for it. This was a Screen Actors Guild signatory commercial, which means that the producers were obliged to hire union performers. Because they were unable to fill the role with a union performer, they were allowed to hire someone who wasn't in the union, even though it would cost them more money, which is called Taft Hartley. As a result, I was eligible to join the union, which can often take years!

I was ready for the big time now and never looked back. That was my first real stunt job even though it would be several more years before I found out that I could really make a living doing exciting work like that. At the time, I did not know what a stuntwoman was or even that they existed. My dream of working in television and movies was born from that day of working on the commercial.

My plan when I'd left for college was to become an orthodontist. That changed when I took an elective theater class at the University of Miami. I had a teacher named Buckets Lowery, and he was an amazing person. He made it fun to learn to act. In one of the first classes, he made us all be trees. I thought that was great! What a cool way to make a living. I loved being on stage and learning to act. Buckets also taught me the importance of being on time. That was a valuable lesson that I never forgot. Soon my days consisted of rehearsing for plays, auditioning for commercials, modeling, and studying. I loved every minute of being at U of M. I was cast in several plays, and there was one critic's review that I always remembered.

He said I moved as though I was a panther in an earlier incarnation. The play was *Funny Thing Happened on the Way to the Forum*, and John Carradine was the guest artist star.

As a sophomore, I was crowned the University of Miami's homecoming queen. Out of 16,774 students, it was quite an honor. And the title led to many more modeling jobs as well. After graduation, I moved home to New Jersey to live with my parents in their beautiful ranch house. I had a sweet, hot-pink room with white furniture adorned with tiny pink rosebuds. I was trying to get work as an actress in New York City. Many doors were slammed in my face. I was not having much luck with getting any jobs. One day when I arrived home after a day of pounding the pavement for hours and countless rejections, my mom said, "Hey, they are opening a Playboy Club in Great Gorge. I think you would make a cute Bunny." So, I called up and made an appointment for my interview.

When the day arrived, with my mother waiting in the car for me as she'd done so many other times at modeling gigs, I confidently pranced into the meeting with the Bunny Mother, Sandy. She was an extremely sweet older woman who looked very well preserved. Her eyelashes were long and fake and her nails the same. She looked stunning. She asked me if I knew how to make drinks, and I told her I had no clue. "Perfect," she said. "You will be starting Bunny School in two weeks, and we will teach you everything you need to know." Wow! Bunny School! How fun! "You will be living in the Bunny Dorm on the property and get chauffeured up to the club every day for class."

Being a Bunny was a blast. Running around in the bunny outfit and making amazing tips was a unique way to make a living. I would still hop into the city on my days off to look for film, television, and modeling work. I could have transferred to the New York City club, but I loved living in the country at the Bunny Dorm. I also got to go horseback riding and skiing on my days off. Life was good, and I enjoyed the glamour of Bunny life. After my best friend Linda and I took a trip to Europe, which I adored, I asked to be transferred to the Playboy Club in London! Although the Bunny Mother informed me that it wouldn't be possible since the company couldn't get me a work visa, I was determined! Not being one to take "no" for answer when it interfered with my dreams, I wrote a letter to the manager of the Playboy Club in London and persuaded him to hire me. Several months later, I received a work permit for the especially skilled job of "Bunny Trainer." And the amazing experience confirmed that I could get any job on which I set my mind.

The day my dad crouched down beside me after I'd been thrown from the mighty Appaloosa, Dynamite, he already knew what I would come to learn from his example and his words: *you can do anything you put your mind to*. We can accomplish anything if we can see it, first, in our minds. I'd also hear similar strains of this powerful truth in *Think and Grow Rich*, which the Deckers would share with me. Climbing back on Dynamite and visualizing myself soaring over the fence that had bested both of us was the first time I'd pause to visualize success, but it wouldn't be the last. In my first drag race, with Lil Sis emblazoned on the side of my vehicle, I could see the burnt orange Corvette as the first car to fly across the finish line. Galloping bareback along a beautiful beach, I could see myself winning the acting role and starring in the commercial we'd film the following week. And when the Bunny Mother told me I could transfer to any location in the United States, but not to London, she couldn't have known that I'd already seen my success at the Playboy Club across the pond!

Maybe you feel stuck right now. If you've not made the decision to pause and visualize your future success, it's possible your engine is idling. When you imagine your future, can you see yourself succeeding in your dream job? In school? At becoming the best you can be? While there's certainly no magic bullet that guarantees success, my experience has taught me that pausing to "see" the success you're after—whether it's clearing a fence, landing a promotion, developing a business, or finally making the decision to pursue that thing that gives your heart joy—is an important step in achieving that success. Someone else's "no" doesn't determine your "yes"! You can accomplish your dreams, but first you have to visualize yourself succeeding. If fear of failure arises, you must deflect it and focus on the prize . . . your dream come true.

During my time in London working at the Playboy Club, I had amazing opportunities to travel to places like Amsterdam, Tunisia, and Turkey. I was making great money and having a blast, but my dream of working in the film business was going nowhere. My work permit was for the Playboy Club only. I knew it was time for me to get home to the States and follow my dream. Dreams change and evolve, and the color of my future was glowing in my head. After almost a year in London, it was time to make a move. The novelty had worn off, and now I was ready to dive head-on into the film business.

3

New York City, Here I Come!

After I'd moved back home to New Jersey to live with my folks, I'd gotten lucky fairly quickly and landed a small acting role on *Kojak*, the television series starring Telly Savalas. My character was named "Woman with a Baby Carriage." I was crossing the street at Seventy-Seventh and Madison with my baby in the carriage when a speeding car being chased by police raced right toward me. Adrenaline coursing through my veins, I let out a blood curdling scream.

The director said, "Let's do it one more time, Diane. Wait a beat longer, then make your exit."

Wow, I loved the rush I got from shooting that scene. Was I afraid that the car might hit me? Yes, but I consciously overcame that fear by visualizing the scene going perfectly right.

During the second take, once again the speeding car careened directly at me. I waited a beat longer and this time the baby carriage was almost a goner!

"Cut, print . . . incredible, Diane," the director beamed.

I was hooked!

I was hired by an extras casting company and just happened to be at the right spot at the right time for the director to ask me to perform a "stunt" like that. Little did I know it was a stunt. I never really heard of stunts before that day. What I did know was that I loved the feeling of that adrenaline rush. Divine order? Miracle of timing? Or just a case of pure destiny that nudged me into a career that blossomed into forty-plus years of mostly pure joy and excitement? A new horizon was before me.

The seed of a dream of doing stunts was planted in me that August day in New York City in 1974.

I raced over to one of the stunt guys who was driving the car that almost hit me. His name was Alex Stevens, and he was the president of the East Coast Stuntmen's Association. Alex was a ruggedly handsome Greek guy in his early forties. He was talking to Harry Madsen, the other stunt driver, also good-looking in a bad boy type way. They had a bag of toy cars, and they were laying them out in the street planning the next part of the car chase. I knew better than to interrupt as they were so intense on moving the tiny cars and discussing where and when they would slide and spin the vehicles. I was amazed. My job was complete, and I was released from the set, but I stayed and watched with glee as Alex and Harry slid through street corners nearly hitting parked cars and everything else in sight. That was the day that I knew stunts were what I wanted to do. I had never, ever thought of that before. It was an epiphany! I approached the two stuntmen with awe while they were on a break drinking coffee, smoking, and laughing about the incredible car chase that I just witnessed.

"Hi, I'm Diane Peterson and I'd really like to do stunts! I ride and jump horses, race my car in the quarter-mile drags, and ride a motorcycle too!" I proudly boasted.

They looked me up and down and Alex blurted out, "Forget it honey, we put the wigs on and we do it ourselves."

That was the seventies in New York City, and that is what they did at the time. Today men are not allowed to double women. There were not too many women who wanted to risk life and limb for the movies back then, but I was undeterred by this bit of information. I now definitely had a dream! I would become a famous Hollywood stuntwoman, and I had a burning desire to succeed.

As I continued to hustle for jobs, I began to get more and more small acting roles. Whenever I saw Alex and Harry on the set, I would try to hang around them and ask, "Wow, how did you do that?"

Alex would brush me off with a smile and say, "Stick to acting, honey."

I would follow them and watch them from afar as they set up stunts and performed them. They looked pretty ridiculous in wigs and ladies' dresses. They didn't seem to care if everyone made fun of them. In fact, I think they enjoyed it! Plus, they were making the big stunt checks and residuals too. I just watched and waited and prayed that one day my chance would come to show them what I could do. I was fearless and confident and felt that stunts were my calling, my dharma, my life's purpose.

Two months later, I got a call from Alex who said he had a job for me. I could not believe he finally was calling me for work. My prayers were answered.

"Great, thanks so much. What do I have to do?" I eagerly inquired.

"You have to get hit by a car! Don't worry, we'll teach you how to do it." he laughed.

It was for a traffic safety film, he explained. Was I scared of getting hit by a car? Damn right I was. But I had blind faith that the guys would teach me and keep me safe. My dad had planted the seed in my mind and heart that I could overcome my fears and do anything I put my mind to. Now was my opportunity. I could hardly sleep with anticipation.

I arrived at daybreak in a small town on Long Island. I was ecstatic and more than thrilled to be called in to do my first "big" stunt with the president of the East Coast Stuntmen's Association. I was nervous but eager. I loved the sensation of my racing heart fueling my adrenaline. Alex and Harry greeted me with hugs and proceeded to explain how the "hit" was going to happen.

I would start walking across the street, minding my own business in a four-lane intersection. The car in the lane closest to me with Harry driving would stop and allow me to pass. I would smile and wave and walk into the next lane where a speeding car, driven by Alex, would race up and hit me. It was all in the timing, or so they said.

We tried it a few times at slow speed. I rolled across the hood of the car and ended up in the windshield. It was as scary as you might expect! I had to really concentrate to overcome the fear of actually getting run over! I kept visualizing the stunt going right. They gave me elbow pads, kneepads and a pad to put on the side of the hip that eventually would hit the ground. I looked enormous with all those pads on, but I listened to their words of wisdom: "You need to wear every pad that you can get away with." The mantra "cover yourself, cover yourself, cover yourself" was drummed into my head that very first day on the set. It was those words that would help me save my butt throughout the years. I never forgot that I should "cover myself!" and when I ignored that advice, I regretted it painfully.

"Ok, we're ready, cameras rolling, action!" I heard the director yell on the bullhorn.

My heart was racing like a steam engine. I sauntered onto the street and noticed the first car coming. He stopped, I smiled, waved, and continued on. The second car came fast! BOOM! It hit me, and I flew onto the hood of the car, slammed into the windshield, and broke it with my elbow. Thank God for the elbow pad. Alex floored the car, and I flew off the hood and landed on the street, stunned. *Whew*, I thought. I made it out alive.

Dazed, I heard the director yell, "Bring in the other car, we are going again."

Yikes! I had to do it again?!

Alex said, "Good job, but don't anticipate."

It is hard not to anticipate when you hear a roaring car about to run you over!

Take two. The first car stopped, and the second car whacked me in the knees! The hood of the car hit me in my knees really, really hard. *The hell with this!*

I was acting and modeling, and I did not need to get hurt. No photographer wanted to shoot my bruises and scars! I picked myself up off the ground and my knees were shaking.

Alex ran over and said, "Are you ok?"

I blurted out, "That's it. I'm done. That really hurt. I'm going home now."

He grabbed me by the shoulders and said, "Look Diane, it's like falling off a horse. If you don't get right back out there and do it again, you will never do another stunt in your life."

Well, obviously he had my attention.

So I went out there, knees shaking, for take three. There's a fine line between bravery and stupidity. I focused my attention, dispelled the fear and *bam!* The car hit was amazing. I could hear the applause from the gathering crowd.

I liked that a lot. Adrenaline married with fear, overcome by the mind's focus, and my action appreciated by the applauding crowd. I could get used to that!

My dad's words echoed in my head and throughout my body, "You can do anything you put your mind to."

Next, I got to drive the car and hit *the guys!* I was right on my mark with the car and at just the correct speed. I didn't run over either one of them. I was now officially in the club, a member of The East Coast Stuntmen's Association. The token female, a budding star, eager to learn all that I could about stunts.

I really loved the car chase aspect of the business. Driving was my thing as far back as I could remember when I took the wheel in the little old pickup truck. I began renting cars from rental agencies to practice sliding them sideways and spinning them in empty parking lots. After all, I didn't want to wreck my own car! Alex was a patient teacher and would put cones around for me to slide up to and stop before I knocked them over. I seemed to have an inborn knack for the timing. My very favorite were the 180-degree turns. I performed them perfectly. I quickly graduated to doing them in reverse. I could floor the car in reverse, cut the wheel, spin, and then drop the car in drive and speed off with the wheels spinning and tires screeching, no problem. I got a thrill beyond words executing these maneuvers. Those poor rental cars—I would return them with worn tires and limping transmissions.

A few weeks later, I got called for my first car job! I was hired to drive the Porsche in the film *Gumball Rally*, and I was confident in my abilities. About fifteen stuntmen from California were flown into New York City for the car chase.

The stunt coordinator from California instructed me, "I want you to barrel ass out of the driveway, slide sideways, and peel off down the street."

We were in a small garage on the Upper East side. I walked the route that I was about to take and noticed that the driveway was quite steep for a low-riding sports car. I thought if I angled my car I would avoid bottoming out. There were several cars ahead of me, all revving their engines and waiting for action. I heard action on the bullhorn. The two cars in front of me shot out of the open garage and the door shut. I was next. My adrenaline was pumping, my hands were sweating, and the garage door flew open. I floored the little Porsche and hit the driveway. Just as I thought, the driveway was way too steep for my low-riding car. As I turned the wheel to slide sideways, I bottomed out and began sliding directly toward a crowd of gaping bystanders and cameraman in the center island of the street. My heart was in my throat as I jumped the curb and saw people scattering. The woman riding passenger with me screamed as I struggled to hold onto the wheel of the nearly out-of-control car. I bounced back down the curb and the car fishtailed and rocketed down the street. I thought I was going to have a heart attack. I could have killed ten people. Another huge lesson was learned: you must listen to your inner voice. I knew that driveway was too steep to barrel out fast. When I returned to the garage, the director said, "That was incredible." I smiled, nodded, and graciously accepted the kudos, acting as if I had the whole maneuver planned. And so it is in stunts. Many times, the action morphs into an event that was not completely planned, and the action on film is amazing. Sadly, sometimes the inevitable occurs and a tragedy strikes, but this time luck was in my favor.

Word got out that I was a "hot shoe," as they call it, meaning I was great behind the wheel. Soon after, I was called for a Woody Allen film, *Annie Hall*. I was to double Diane Keaton in a driving sequence in New York City and slide a Volkswagen beetle into a tiny parking space sideways. At the interview, Woody was sitting there in enormous glasses looking much smaller than I imagined him to be. I was a bit nervous meeting him, but I rose above the feeling, smiled big and introduced myself.

Woody queried, "Can you drive?"

I assured him, "I'm a dynamite driver, the best."

"You got the job."

I arrived on the set early one sizzling summer morning. I noticed that I was sharing a dressing room with Diane Keaton. My name was on the door beneath hers. I really did not know who she was except that she was the star and that I was doubling her. She was super nice to me and thanked me in advance for doing the driving sequences. I had to giggle inside when I saw the funky outfit that I had to wear. I emerged from the dressing room looking, in my opinion, like a refugee, but that was Annie Hall.

I hopped into the VW Beetle and asked to take it around the block a few times in order to get the feel of the brakes and the wheel.

Seeing Woody, I invited him to join me, "Hop in."

He stammered, "Oh no, I'm afraid to ride passenger on this crazy ride. You are taking my double."

His photo double jumped in the car and started chatting like a noisy parrot. I told him to put his seat belt on and shut up. Ha! It was my time to concentrate, and I did not need his distractions. I also had a cameraman in the back seat filming the action.

On Woody's command of "Action," I began weaving in and out of traffic, driving erratically. I could see the white knuckles of my frightened passenger. Then all of a sudden a guy stepped out in the street from between two parked cars. *Oh, what the hell,* I thought, *I'll just aim at him and make him part of the scene.* He jumped back like a scared rat. I floored the car and took off uptown. I slid sideways around a corner and saw the tiny parking space ahead where I was supposed to land. I focused on the mantra, "Keep your eyes fixed on where you want the car to go."

I locked up the wheels and slid sideways right to the curb! Whew!

"That was amazing, Diane," Woody yelled.

I was feeling pumped and proud when a police officer appeared and reamed me.

"Don't you ever aim at a pedestrian again! You could have killed him."

Ashamed, I looked down and said, "I'm so sorry, it just kinda happened. He stepped out in front of me." I began to realize that there could be a fine line between getting the shot and losing a life.

When I'd first told Alex Stevens, president of the East Coast Stuntmen's Association, that I wanted to do stunts, he'd brushed me off. And while I'd like to attribute my success to my excellent stunt skills and natural charisma, Alex ended up being an important person on my journey. I followed everything Alex and Harry did, learning all I could, and eventually Alex called to offer me a job. Not only did he offer me the job, but he also coached me through the whole stunt. And when I stumbled and fell? Alex was at my side encouraging me to keep going. From setting up orange cones in empty parking lots to showing me which protective pads to use, Alex's support was critical to my success.

Notice the people in your path who might help you achieve your dreams. Look for mentors who are doing the thing you dream of doing and glean what you can. Study them. Learn from mistakes they made. And let them introduce you to others who can help you take the next step in your journey. If you're a creative person and dream of freelancing, meet with a friend who's savvy about the business end of things. If your dream requires extra training or education, talk to someone who's traveled that path. Nurture the relationships that will equip you to be the person you were made to be and do the thing you were made to do. And if you're really lucky, you might get to meet a kind and wise mentor! It would be a few years before I had the opportunity to help others the way Alex had helped me, but that day was coming.

Annie Hall was the first of many of my films to win an Academy Award. I am pleased to know that I had something to do with that!

4

It Was a Man's World

"Diane, how would you like to learn how to do a high fall? I have this brand-new invention called an airbag. The fire department is going to be out with their fire truck for me to demonstrate how it works."

While I can see how a lot of women wouldn't get excited about this kind of an invitation, even from a handsome young stuntman, the Saturday morning phone call from stuntman A.J. Bakunas both thrilled and terrified me! A.J. was rugged and well-built and resembled a young Karl Malden. Everyone flocked around him to hear his stories of incredible high falls that he performed in unusual places around the Metropolitan area of New York City. And though we were both about twenty-four years old and had a bit of an attraction for each other, I had a self-imposed rule that I would not get involved in a relationship with any stuntman. I wanted to be known for my work and not for who I slept with.

The challenges facing a woman trying to get a foot in the door of the stuntman's boys' club was, in many ways, no different from the challenges faced by women climbing the ladder in other industries. I knew I had the spirit and the drive. And I knew that I wanted to be in the movie business, but did I have the courage to overcome my fears? After all, I was an ex-Playboy Bunny, sexy, feminine, and now I was also modeling and acting. What lured me into this dangerous, sometimes frightening, venture? I needed to dig deep and find out why I had this insatiable desire to overcome my fears. There were no stuntwomen working in New York City at the time, so against all odds, I was the first. I flashed back to being the only girl trumpet player in grammar school. The boys teased me mercilessly because I played first trumpet. They wanted to play first trumpet. Would this venture be a repeat torture? I was soon to find out.

A. J. Bakunas, who'd phoned me about an opportunity to learn to do high falls, was known for his high falls. In fact, his nickname was "The Gentleman Jumper." Before the airbag, high falls were done into stacks of cardboard boxes piled on top of each other with a mat on top. *Oh my God,* I thought to myself, *I don't want to learn this . . . I hate heights.* But I knew if I wanted to continue on to be a great stuntwoman, I would have to master this nagging trepidation.

I wanted to be in the boys' club, and this was an invitation that I could not pass up.

From the moment that I hung up the phone, I kept hearing my mother's haunting words, "Don't go near the edge, Diane. Don't go near the edge." The seed of fear had been firmly planted in my fertile brain. Yes, anyone in their right mind *should* be afraid of falling from a height! But my mom had also watered and nurtured that little seed.

I arrived at the scene, located A.J. and Alex, and saw the fire truck surrounded by a dozen good-looking macho firemen.

A.J. didn't waste any time and said, "Let's go." I followed him and Alex and jumped into the cherry picker of the fire truck. Up we went, and as I looked down, the airbag began to look smaller and smaller. My nerves were porcupine quills racing up and down my spine. I found myself fifty feet up in the air staring at the fifteen-by-fifteen-foot airbag that now appeared to look like a postage stamp. Being flanked by these two talented stuntmen did nothing to relieve my anxiety. Huge fans were blowing air into the vents in the bag to keep it full. Everyone was staring up at us as my knees were shaking. I tried to remain cool and calm despite the inner turmoil.

Suddenly, A.J. and Alex said, "See ya," and both jumped out of the tiny cage leaving me stranded at the top alone.

Was this some kind of cruel joke? Why are they torturing me? I yearned to disappear into thin air.

A.J. and Alex were yelling at me, "Come on, come on, jump!"

"No way, bring me down!" I hollered back.

I was frozen to the floor of the cherry picker with fear. There was no way in hell that I was going to jump. I pleaded with them to lower the cage, and finally they slowly brought me down to about twenty-five feet from the bag, though they were laughing their asses off at my expense. I did not find the situation in the least bit funny.

In unison, they began to shout instructions at me. "Tuck your head, jump, and land flat out on your back."

Oh my God, it still looks so high. Why am I doing this? But there was no other way down. Inhaling a deep breath, I took the plunge. It seemed like I was falling for an eternity. Whack! I landed flat out on my back and the bag gave way like a giant marshmallow. On impact, the air was knocked out of me, but only briefly. I was enveloped by the bag and the guys pulled me out to the ground. I survived the first of many high falls in my career.

Like madmen, the boys said, "OK, let's go higher!"

Reluctantly, I agreed and continued jumping higher and higher, just to prove to them that I could do it. I mastered the task that day, but the fear lingered on and still exists to this day. Overcoming the fear while performing the stunt was a skill that I was perfecting.

Sadly, a few years later A.J. Bakunas, The Gentleman Jumper, died doing a high fall. He was trying to set the world high fall record. He went through the bag when he jumped from the twenty-third floor, 323 feet up off the Kincaid Towers in Lexington, Kentucky in 1978.

I was still living at home in New Jersey and trying to get more work in the movie business when I got a call to work on the remake of *King Kong*. I talked to my dad about the stunt that I had to do. I had to run along the third rail of the subway track where it was elevated above the street. Then I had to climb down a forty-foot emergency ladder attached to the iron girders in an evening dress and high heels! My dad dragged out the forty-foot ladder we had in the garage and stuck it in a tree in our backyard. It was a hot, steamy, summer day in Jersey, and I began running up and down the ladder in my high heels as fast as I could. My dad knew that I was sketchy about heights, and he had the brilliant idea for me to practice in the comfort of our backyard.

Dad said, "Make sure you stay on the balls of your feet and don't look down, honey."

Within moments my mom came running out the back door, all red in the face yelling, "What are you doing, Diane? You are going to fall and break your neck."

"Don't worry Mom, I'm practicing for a big stunt that I have to do tonight in New York City," I calmly explained.

"Please don't do that, you don't need to hurt yourself," she pleaded.

"Oh Mom, I'll be all right, please don't worry. And please do not come to watch the filming. I don't want you to be worried and scared."

Up and down the ladder I went until I felt I had mastered it.

I arrived on the set at a busy intersection in New York City where the subway went up over the street in a section called the L. The street was beginning to get closed off to traffic and the onlookers were gathering. I went to my dressing room and found a long-beaded sequin gown hanging there with an extremely high-heeled pair of shoes parked beneath it. I squeezed into the gorgeous dress and balanced in the sky-high stilettos. I strutted my way over to the hair and makeup trailer. There I met Jessica Lange whom I would be doubling.

Jessica smiled and said, "Hello, you must be my stunt double." Her hair was shorter than mine and I noticed a blond wig perched on a Styrofoam head. The hairdresser lady asked me to take a seat and began digging bobby pins into my scalp. She plopped the wig on my head and secured it with hundreds of pins. The makeup artist threw some base makeup, powder, and red lipstick on me, and I was ready to roll.

I ventured out to the set in my new "look" with male heads spinning one-eighties to glimpse a look at the "sexy" blond. The tight sequined dress really accentuated my fit, lithe body. The scene in *King Kong* was an exciting one. I would be running along the high voltage rail—of course, the power would be turned off. I hoped. Then I would climb down the forty-foot emergency ladder to the pavement below. Jeff Bridges would be running in front me, or it would be his stuntman. We rehearsed the action many times at slow speed, and I was ready. An enormous crowd gathered behind the barricades and police were holding them back.

The director, John Guillermin, yelled on the bullhorn, "Action, Diane."

I ran as fast as I could in the extremely tight dress and horrible high-heel shoes that were killing my feet. I was nervous, but I would not let my fear of heights rear its ugly head. I focused on the task ahead, descending the daunting ladder.

"Faster, faster, Diane" the director yelled on the bullhorn.

The heel of my shoe kept getting caught in the hem of my dress. I struggled to get free. I thought, You *put this dress on and try running down this ladder!* My father's words, "Don't look down, don't look down," echoed in my mind. My heart was beating so fast I thought it would jump right out of my skin. My palms were sweating as I raced down the ladder to safety.

"Let's go again, Diane. Faster this time," John barked.

The wardrobe lady taped up the hem of my dress so on the second take I was able to move more swiftly down the ladder. Faster and faster I descended, almost stepping on the stuntman's hands beneath me. I hit the pavement and began running—after all, King Kong was chasing me!

"Cut, that's a print, we've moving on. Fantastic job, Diane." John smiled.

I don't blame my mom for the fear I felt when standing precariously forty or fifty feet up in the air! Fear is the appropriate response to certain situations, and this was one of them. But I had to decide, and you have to decide, whether or not we will be bullied by our fear. Will it keep us from doing the thing we want to do? Will it prevent us from reaching the dreams we have in our hearts? I believe that each one of us has the choice whether we will be mastered by our fears or whether we will master them.

I've been pretty purposeful to not let my fears keep me from reaching my dreams. Choosing to jump into an airbag from twenty-five feet—and then thirty and then forty—was a choice I made to not let fear control me. Scrambling up and down a backyard ladder in heels was another way to master my fear by honing my skillset so that I'd be well prepared.

I had the power to reject fear and move forward toward success, and you do, too. Maybe you've been procrastinating about turning in the application for the training you need to take for your next step. Or perhaps you're afraid that you don't have what it takes to achieve the dream that's bubbling in your heart. Or maybe, like me, you're anxious about taking a big leap of faith! You have to leave what's secure in order to step forward into what feels like a free fall. I want you to hear that you can choose to reject fear by taking the next step in your journey toward success. Maybe that step is making one phone call. Or maybe it's jumping off a building. When you choose to reject fear, you can achieve your dreams.

I'm delighted to report that I outran King Kong that day in the sequined dress. And after the director shouted cut, I turned toward the crowd applauding feverously and saw my mom standing there holding my dad's hand and smiling. I could not believe that she actually came to watch this terrifying scene. She was proud of me, and I was proud of her.

She hadn't let fear be the boss of her.

5

California Dreaming

A mysterious-looking gypsy woman, with bells on her ankles and a colorful scarf tied around her waist, approached the table at the Gypsy Tea Room in Manhattan where my mom and I had dropped armfuls of shopping bags, filled with too many pairs of pretty high-heeled shoes, and collapsed into our chairs.

"May I read your tea leaves when you are finished drinking your tea?" she asked with a smile and a wink.

I looked at my mom and she nodded yes so, I said, "OK, why not?"

We drank our tea and talked about our shoes and how we couldn't wait to show them to my dad. I signaled the gypsy when we were through, and she sashayed over to our table and sat down rather close. She swirled the remaining drops of tea around and around in my cup and peered intently at the leaves resting at the bottom of the cup.

Looking directly in my eyes she announced, "I see that you are going on a long journey by car and that you will be living by the sea."

My mother burst into tears.

I said, "Yes, yes, I've been planning on moving to California. In fact, I am leaving in August."

"This is where you must go," the gypsy smiled and drifted away.

It was July of 1976, and I was twenty-five years old. I knew that I had to move to California if I was ever going to really "make it" in the film and television business. New York was great for theater, soaps, and television commercials, but I had a dream to do much more. The only action television show was *Kojak*. I had worked on that show repeatedly, and it was winding down. There were only a few feature films that would shoot in New York and the surrounding areas. When a feature film came to New York City that originated in California, they would bring California stuntpeople with them for the best stunts. The New Yorkers were left with the crumbs.

Hollywood, though, was the film capital of the world. I had been California dreamin' for a long, long time. I had worked in New York City for two years and I felt I had enough stunt experience and plenty of good credits on my résumé. I was confident that I could find work and follow my dream to become a top Hollywood stuntwoman. My only reservation was that I would be far away from my folks. I loved them dearly, and we were very close. One morning after breakfast, I told my dad about my plan to go west.

Squeezing me in a big bear hug, he reassured me, "Go for it, baby. You'll only be a plane ride away."

My dad always taught me that I could do anything that I put my mind to. His joyful spirit and kind ways made it wonderful to be in his presence.

My mom was a completely different story, and she sobbed when I told her about my plan to move out west. I reassured her that everything was going to be okay and told her not to worry. Little chance of that!

When I told Alex Stevens, my mentor, that I was moving to Los Angeles he begged, "Don't do that Diane, you are the only stunt girl we have in New York, we need you. Why don't you fly out there and see if you like it?"

"I know I'm going to like it," I blurted out.

I felt it deep in my psyche. It was flattering to be needed. I knew that I had the market cornered in New York, but the winter was rapidly approaching, and there was not much stunt work in the city at that time of year. It was time to go.

My new shoes would soon have a brand-new home in Los Angeles.

In my little pink bedroom, I agonized over what I could squeeze into a few small suitcases that would fit into my 1968 Orange Bronze 350-horsepower, four-speed Corvette with a T-top. What a hot car I had! I knew I would have to pack wisely, especially to fit all those shoes in my car! I tried in vain to find anyone brave enough to make the move to the West Coast with me. I was determined to "follow my dream," and I got a stack of maps from the Auto Club with a planned route to my undiscovered future in LA I was listening to the Beach Boys album *Surfin' Safari* and imagining where I would live.

My cute pink Princess phone rang, and it was a voice that I was always glad to hear. Dave was calling from Miami to see how

I was doing. Dave Heimann was a college boyfriend of mine. I called him a "beefcaker." He was constantly working out and perfecting his bronze tan. He was tall, blond, and had a body like the statue of David. He liked to call me yacht face because he said I looked like I belonged on a huge yacht. The name sort of stuck. With him, that is. I dated Dave for most of my freshman year in college at the University of Miami. He became obsessed with me, followed me everywhere, and I finally had to break it off. I knew that it was painful for him, and I tried to remain friends.

I told Dave I was moving to LA, and he sheepishly asked who I was driving out there with.

"No one," I answered. "I'm going alone."

Dave immediately blurted out, "Let me fly up and drive across the country with you. I'll fly back to Miami after you get settled in LA OK?"

Why not? He was good company, and we did have a lot of laughs together. He offered to share the expenses, too.

I ordered, "Great, but you can only bring one small bag."

The day we launched from New Jersey, Dave had a pad and pencil and explained to me that he would keep track of everything we spent, and I mean everything—even a pack of gum! We would then split the cost of the trip. I was fine with that and happy to have a navigator and friend with me for the journey. I did most of the driving because: (a) I liked driving a lot; (b) it was my car; and (c) I was a better driver! We stopped whenever and wherever we wanted and were in no particular hurry to reach the West Coast. If there was a scenic spot, we would pull over and enjoy the moment.

We cruised into Hollywood on a sizzling summer day in August 1976. Sunset Boulevard, with the impressive billboards and enormous swaying palm trees, welcomed my arrival. I envisioned that one of the movies I would work on would be on one of those billboards. We checked into a penthouse suite at the Holiday Inn to celebrate and sipped champagne as we stared at the lights of the city. I wondered where I would find my first apartment and where my first job would come from. I had faith that I would be led in the right direction. I only knew one friend, Jan Zipp, a sorority sister from Tri Delta at the University of Miami. She lived in Huntington Beach, which was quite far from the Los Angeles area. It was comforting just to know that she was there.

I'd read an article about Marina Del Rey, a swinging singles paradise that sounded fabulous to me. After all, I was only twenty-five, single, and wanted to live by the beach. The marina was also close to the airport in case I was working on movies out of town.

Dave had to get back to law school in Miami, so early the next morning, I dropped him off at the airport. We hugged and kissed, and I knew that I would not be seeing him for a long, long time. He was madly in love with me, but I just did not feel the same way about him. I valued our friendship, and I knew that I would miss the laughs and hugs, but it was time to begin my new life in this vast incredible territory.

I drove to Marina Del Rey and marveled at the enormous yachts and all the people riding bikes, running, and enjoying life. I immediately knew this was the place for me. I searched the tiny roads in the marina by the sea and came upon an apartment complex called Mariners Village. It was like fantasia. The nautical-style complex had ponds with giant koi fish the size of barracuda swimming around. Wooden bridges, captain's lanterns, and lush greenery enveloped the tropical landscape. I was in heaven. The agent took me to a furnished studio apartment on a street called Northwest Passage. The unit was tiny but cute and had a rather large balcony. It had two twin beds that doubled as sofas and a built-in desk and bookshelves. The itty-bitty kitchen even had a dishwasher—something my mother never wanted. The balcony overlooked a gorgeous, green courtyard with beautiful orange flowers. A sweet fragrance filled the air, and I felt that I was home, sweet home.

Before I left New Jersey, I'd ordered my parents a new white Chevrolet Monte Carlo. I had saved enough for the down payment and got a loan from the bank for the balance. It would arrive there for my parent's fortieth wedding anniversary in November. I was so confident that I would find work and be successful that I took the plunge and ordered the car. My parents had always put my brother's and my needs before theirs, and I wanted to surprise them big time for their very special fortieth anniversary. So, besides my new rent, I had a car payment to make!

Somehow, I knew I'd be able to handle both.

I began feverously sending out pictures and résumés. My enthusiasm and positive attitude driven by my dream of being successful in Hollywood propelled my desire to find work. I had a list of stunt coordinators, agents, casting directors, and an enormous supply of pictures and résumés. I gave myself the nickname "Dynamite Diane," and every day I would take my stack of correspondence, pictures, résumés, and letters asking for work or an interview to the post office. Then I would go to the beach and fantasize about working on a movie doing incredible stunts. I would try to conjure up a job in my head. I'd visualize myself going to MGM, Paramount, Universal, and 20th Century Fox and reporting for work. I would gaze at my surroundings, the beautiful beach, the birds flying in formation, and listen to the waves and laugh to myself. If I had to be out of work for the moment, this is one incredible place to be. It was so unlike pounding the pavement in New York City looking for my next break.

There were no cell phones or answering machines in those days, so I didn't want to be away from the telephone for too long. One morning, a modeling agency from Hollywood called me. I had sent them my picture and figured I could always model to bring in a few bucks before I got my big break. The agency wanted to see me immediately, so I picked out a cute, sexy outfit; high heels; short, tight skirt; and colorful, revealing top. I was lookin' good. I curled my long blond hair and did my makeup perfectly. I hopped in my little orange Corvette and headed out for Hollywood. *Sunset Boulevard, here I come,* I thought as I followed my trusty map into town. I parked my Corvette on Sunset Boulevard, ran across the street, and hopped in the elevator.

A guy in a gray business suit got in the elevator with me and said, "Excuse me, are you a stuntwoman?"

I said, "Yeah, how did you know that?"

He said he parked behind me and saw my East Coast Stuntmen's Association sticker in my rear window.

He said, "I think you would make a great double for Deborah Raffin. Can you drive?"

With confidence I assured him, "I'm a dynamite driver, I'm the best."

He asked me to come to his office after my interview and meet the stunt coordinator, Conrad Palmisano. His office was in the same building, a few floors below the agency.

The interview with the modeling agency went well. They wanted to sign me and send me out on some upcoming job interviews. I then marched down a few floors to the production office for

Assault in Paradise, a.k.a. *The Ransom*, and met Conrad Palmisano. He asked me if I could drive, and you know the answer!

I immediately replied, "I'm a dynamite driver, I'm the best!"

"Okay, we're going to Arizona. You will be doubling Deborah Raffin, and we'll be doing plenty of car chases," Conrad explained.

I didn't know who Deborah Raffin was, but it didn't matter to me.

"Cool, I'm ready, when do we leave?"

Conrad explained that we would be leaving in a week.

Wow, I am in!

I could hardly believe my good fortune. I'd always heard how important it was to be in the right place at the right time, and at last I was! Some might call it destiny, or even coincidence, but I knew God was on my side.

While it's not always possible to be in "the right place" at "the right time," you can always do your part to help destiny along. In different moments, I'd had to trust the little voice inside me about what the right next move was going to be. Had I heeded my mom's fear, I would have stayed in New Jersey. And even if I'd been flattered by Alex's confidence in me, I'd still have been in New York and not in that fortuitous elevator in Hollywood! By packing up my little Vette and driving across the country to relocate in the Los Angeles area, I'd done what I could to be in the right place. As far as the right "time," maybe I got a *little* lucky to have someone park behind me and notice the East Coast Stuntmen's Association sticker in my rear window!

When opportunities present themselves, be ready to seize them. Carry business cards to share with the folks you meet in elevators, on subway cars, and in fancy restaurants. These days it's necessary to have an online presence so that the right people can discover you. If you dream of being an Olympic skier, live by the slopes in Colorado or Utah. And if you want to be a surf star, live by the big waves in Hawaii. Begin making the choices now that will position you to capitalize on opportunities that present themselves.

Finally living in California was as satisfying as I imagined it would be. My dream was coming true: I was about to start working in stunts in Los Angeles.

6

My Dreams Unfolding

Arriving in Phoenix I was eager to start driving. On the first day of the shoot, I was riding as a passenger in the back seat of a Caddy convertible. There were three of us in the back seat and two in the front seat. The driver on action was to do a 180-degree turn with the Caddy, and we were all holding on for dear life. The stunt went perfectly and there was a cut, so we all relaxed.

The driver, trying to be funny, decided he was going to spin the car again to get back to the starting point for a second take. He spun the car and hit a log that was laying at the side of the road. Luckily, the three of us in the back seat fell over, because the log shot up in the air and landed across the back seat of the car right where our heads would have been. I learned a huge lesson that day: don't screw around with the cars when you are not filming! Stunts are not all fun and games. People can and do get hurt.

The rest of the shoot was amazing. Car chases are choreographed like a ballet, and Conrad Palmisano was excellent with his stunt coordination. Waking up each day before my alarm went off, I raced the cars around in the desert, sliding in the dust and dirt and loving every minute of it. I had a lead foot and put the pedal to the metal. Fearless behind the wheel, I could keep chase with the best of them. I was truly living my dream. In fact, there was no question in my mind that this was my purpose in life.

The evenings were party, party, party. The adrenaline had been pumping all day, so the booze flowed freely at night. The guys liked to do these flaming shooters. They would light the whiskey on fire in a shot glass and throw it back down their throats. They teased and taunted me to do a flaming shooter, so reluctantly, I agreed. I nervously tied my hair back and prepared to shoot one. They lit the whiskey on fire and instead of throwing it back down my throat, I touched my lip with the scalding glass and burned my lip really badly. Needless to say, that was the last time I ever attempted to do a flaming shooter!

We worked in Arizona for a couple of weeks, and I didn't want the job to end. Working with great guys, living in a hotel, getting per diem, and eating out, I was having the time of my life. I formed some deep friendships and we vowed to work together again soon. I hoped and prayed that would come true. My mentor, Alex Stevens, used to say, "You are always as good as your last job." The last one had been good, and I was eager for the next.

When I returned to Los Angeles, I began to feverously send out more pictures and résumés. I loved working and I wanted more. My dream wanted to be fed, and I could not rest until I had another job. It is such a joy to find the job that you were meant to have, but the waiting between jobs is the hardest part. It is said that if you find the job you really love, you never really work a day in your life. That is how I felt about stunts.

Back in the seventies, the strategy for getting jobs was to send out a tremendous number of envelopes containing your picture, résumé, and cover letter. Today the process is a whole lot easier and less expensive: you just email your information and attach your photo.

One day, in response to one of my mailings, I got a phone call from a ruff-tuff-sounding kind of guy.

"Diane," he began, "this is Bill Lane." He was a well-known stunt coordinator at that time. One of the unit production managers on *Kojak*, in New York, had given me his address.

Bill asked, "Have you ever been hit by a car?"

"Yes," I assured him, "I can do the best car hit you have ever seen!"

"Okay then," he answered, "you're coming to Nashville. The production office will call you with your flight information."

I'm going to Nashville!

The show was called *Nashville 99*. I packed my stunt bag, which I affectionately called my "Red Bag of Courage," full of every protective pad that I owned. Kneepads, elbow pads, hip pads, and my stunt girdle to hold everything in place. It was a Screen Actors Guild union rule at the time that the production company had to fly you first class. I liked that a lot. I felt like a real star.

A chubby, smiling chauffer was holding a sign with my name on it at the edge of the airport baggage area. I felt so proud carrying my stunt bag and anticipating my new job.

"Hi, young lady!" he cooed. "So you're the stuntwoman. Welcome to Nashville."

We arrived at the Hilton and in the lobby a friendly looking, rugged cowboy in his fifties stuck out his hand.

"Hi, I'm Bill Lane. Drop your things in your room and we are going to look at the location."

Bill had a real man's handshake that gripped my paw like he meant it. I was feeling on top of the world.

As we drove to the location, Bill told me that I would be doubling a hooker and that there would not be much room for pads, if any, in my skimpy wardrobe. I would also be running in super high heels.

"Not a problem," I said.

I was young and invincible and had grown up balancing on pointe shoes in ballet class. Bill and I walked to the site where they'd be shooting the scene. Printers Alley is in downtown Nashville and is home to a nightclub district that dates back to the 1940s. It is a very narrow alley.

In preparation for filming the following day, Bill chased me down the alley in a car as I ran for my life and finally collided with the vehicle. We rehearsed the timing of the car hit a number of times and I told Bill I was good to go. I was extremely glad that we went there to work things out the day before the entire cast and crew arrived. Bill was a very caring and professional stuntman.

The next morning, I was up at the crack of dawn, well before the ordered wakeup call. At the wardrobe department, I was handed a very short, short red skirt, cami top, fishnet hose, and super spike heels. It quickly became clear that there was nowhere to hide my trusted pads.

I reasoned, "I'll just go for it and give them one hell of a hit and maybe I won't have to do it again!"

The logic seemed sound.

Then I found out that I had to wait until dark to do the stunt. The wardrobe department just wanted to be sure that I fit into the clothes and that's why they called me to the set early in the morning. *Ugh!* The waiting was the hardest part. Anticipating the what-ifs and visualizing the perfect outcome were all part of my preparation, as well as remaining focused, and praying, too.

That evening, I arrived on the set looking like a Forty-Second Street hooker from New York City.

Bill took one glance, laughed, and said, "Let's do this."

We did a slow-motion rehearsal so the cameramen could pull focus and get ready to film the action. Then we returned back to the starting position. Cameras rolling, the director yelled, "Action!"

I raced down the street as fast as I could in those lousy high heels. I could hear the car gaining on me, engine getting louder and louder, my heart pounding—NOW!—I spun around and flung myself onto the hood of the speeding car at precisely the right moment. Bill cut the wheel and sent me flying off the hood of the car into the wall of the narrow alley. I hit the wall hard and fell to the ground.

I laid there motionless, thinking to myself, *Am I okay?*

I didn't know yet.

The moment the director yelled "Cut!" the medics rushed in and helped me up.

"Are you okay?" they asked.

"Yes," I said shaking off the dirt. Without hesitation I asked, "Are we going again?"

My knees and elbows were scraped and bleeding, but I was ready to give them another shot.

The director ran over and said, "Oh my God, Diane, that was unbelievable. That's a print, we're movin' on."

Bill put his arm around me and said, "Way to go, girl." I was now on his "A" list for sure.

I was at the right place at the right time, and I'd been able to deliver the goods.

My next movie was *Grand Theft Auto*. Ronnie Howard—known to America as cute little Opie from *The Andy Griffith Show*—would be directing his first film, and I was thrilled to be working with him. He was all grown up and ready to direct this action picture. Vic Rivers and Conrad Palmisano were the stunt coordinators, and they asked me to go to Victorville, California, for a few weeks to double Nancy Morgan and do ND (non-descript stunts).

I agreed without hesitation. I loved working with our little group on that set. Vic Rivers was a little, wiry dynamo guy with big glasses, a mop of dark hair, and a smile that wouldn't quit. Vic previously worked with the Joie Chitwood Thrill Show, so he was well seasoned in executing extraordinary car stunts. Conrad Palmisano was a fearless jokester who could handle anything. Dana Bertolette, a tall, lanky guy with a huge grin, was another Thrill Show driver, and Bruce Barbour was a big, sweet, clown of a guy who always kept me laughing.

A 1959 Rolls Royce was the real star of the show. Most of the time I would ride as a passenger, doubling Nancy Morgan in a hideous brown wig. Dana Bertolette did most of the driving, and he was excellent at sliding that big, heavy vehicle sideways. Riding passenger is much tougher than driving. It requires trusting the guy at the wheel and not screaming when there are close calls. And there were plenty of them! I also rode passenger-side high in the Rolls Royce on the day when Timmy Chitwood put the car on two wheels! He was so good at putting a car on two wheels that it seemed like he was Sunday driving. All the while I was hanging from my seat belt in the passenger seat!

I finally got to drive the Rolls with a helicopter chasing me. Vic was riding passenger in the helicopter as it buzzed by me. I could hear his careful direction on the radio with the pilot. Vic always watched out for me, like a big brother. Dana was riding shotgun with me and never said a word. That's the perfect kind of passenger when you're concentrating. I slid the big beast all over the desert and, in the script, wound up at a country fair that was having a demolition derby. Wow! It was another dream come true to drive in a demolition derby!

I got to decorate one of the cars, an old Plymouth beater, with my newly created name, "Dynamite Diane," spraypainted on the hood and doors. I loved my new nickname! We choreographed the ballet of crashing cars by walking on foot where each car would smash into another on action. We planned this entire sequence in great detail, and then we put our helmets and seat-belts on and were ready to go. My heart was beating furiously when I heard the magic word: "Action." I slammed into the first car, which was an old Dodge, and busted his radiator. Then I got rear-ended by a beat-up Caddy. I retaliated by T-boning a heap of a Chevy. Complete mayhem ensued and cars were smashing all around me—smoking engines, screeching tires, twisted metal. Finally, my car died, and I was a sitting duck. I saw a big old boat of a Lincoln coming my way and I braced for the hit. I heard Ronnie yelling "Cut" on the radio, but it was too late. The Lincoln rammed my door and knocked me across the seat. No seat belts in that old car! I was stunned and slowly began to move my fingers and toes, neck, and shoulders and crawl out of the passenger window. All the drivers were whooping and hollering and trying to tell their story of who hit whom. It all happened so fast! I was laughing so hard that I cried. The guys picked me up and put me on the hood of the smashed car for a group photo. It was a boys' club, and I was proud to be a part of it. Getting and giving respect were paramount in building healthy working relationships.

The day on Printers Alley when Bill Lane careened into me, throwing my body against the wall of the narrow alley, was a pivotal one in my career. In that critical—painful!—moment, I had given the stunt everything I had. And because I'd delivered, Bill was able not only to hire me again, but to recommend me to other stunt coordinators. I'd put in the preparation, I'd stayed focused, and so when the opportunity I'd been so hungry for presented itself, I was *ready*.

As you imagine the kind of life you're after, make sure you've put the building blocks in place that position you for success. If you need the degree, find a way to earn it. If your dream requires a special skill, master it. If you have to build your platform—your social media following, your mailing list, your speaking gigs—then build it. Finding success and joy while living your best life happens when you're prepared to seize the critical opportunity when it presents itself. Get ready to win!

7

Hi-Riders

As the emergency room door swung wide open, I saw my dear friend Vic River's body laying lifeless on the table. Tubes, wires, and pumps were all attached to his ashen frame. Doctors and nurses scrambled to save his precious life. As the rest of the crew and I sat in the waiting room crying and praying, one thought tormented me.

Why did I put Vic's name in for this job?

The film was called *Hi-Riders,* and it was my first starring role as an actress. I played Lynn Morgan, a vivacious, smart aleck blond, who raced cars for money with her boyfriend on the streets of Los Angeles. The role fit me to a T. I wore tight blue jeans tucked into my tan leather high-heel boots. I had a sexy gold chain with a pocket watch tucked inside my jean pocket. My plaid fitted shirt was tied at the midriff and my hair was long, blond, tousled, and layered, Farrah Fawcett style. I looked hot, no two ways about it.

After I was cast, I asked who the stunt coordinator was going to be.

When the director, Greydon Clark, mentioned the name of a guy that I never heard of, I said, "Why don't you interview Vic Rivers and Conrad Palmisano for the job?"

I told him that we had done several car pictures together and that they were amazing stunt coordinators. Greydon agreed to meet them, and the rest is history. Vic and Connie (as Conrad liked to be called) got the job, and I was thrilled to be able to help my buddies get some work.

My costar was Darby Hinton, a tall, blond, extremely well-built, blue-eyed Adonis. We made a gorgeous couple, and sparks flew as we did our scenes together. Greydon kept nodding in approval and biting his lower lip and almost falling off his chair as Darby and I performed our scenes. It was great fun having a starring role because I got my very own trailer and someone available to fix my makeup and hair all day long. I had wardrobe ladies fussing over everything I was going to wear. I was born to play Lynn Morgan as she was just my style. As a result, lots of the clothes and jewelry that I wore on set were my own.

Each day I was prepared for my scenes. After all, I was a graduate of the University of Miami Drama Department! Darby and I had great chemistry and it was a joy to go to the set. We filmed a lot at the Paramount Ranch and in the hilly, winding roads of Agoura and Calabasas, California.

We used to have a funny saying, "The hell with the dialogue, let's wreck something!" And that I did. I got to do a ramp jump in a Camaro through an enormous picture window with a fully loaded fish tank behind it. The morning of the stunt, the other actress who was riding passenger with me was extremely nervous. In fact, she was scared to death when she saw the task at hand. I reassured her and told her not to worry but to just sit still and shut up. I didn't need her nervous energy to distract me. I could see through the window that there was a man with a rifle sitting in a chair in front of the fish tank about to shoot my boyfriend, Darby. The man in the chair was actually a dummy that was about to be flattened by me. On action, I floored the gas pedal and hit the ramp. It all seemed to be happening in slow motion as I crashed through the giant window shattering the glass and the fish tank too! Fish were flying through the air as I crashed down hard on top of the desk. The dummy was crushed like a pancake. I slammed on the brakes, slid to a stop, jumped out of the car, and hugged Darby. I saved his life, and the movie was over with a very happy ending. But a movie is rarely shot in sequence, and we had one bigger stunt left to do.

Vic Rivers was to race an old pickup truck down a bumpy road and do a ramp jump into a small lake. Conrad and Vic both wanted to do the stunt because it was extra money for the stunt adjustment, besides being a huge thrill. So, they flipped a coin and Vic won. I went to talk to Vic before the stunt. Because I am Catholic, I tried to give Vic a Saint Christopher medal to put in his pocket for safety, good luck, and blessings.

But he said lightheartedly, "Aw, I don't need that, Diane. See you on the other side."

I gave him a big hug and went on my way.

The pickup truck was old and rusty and had a crappy suspension. It bounced along like a rambling wreck. Vic had removed the back window of the pickup truck and rolled the windows down. Conrad wanted him to take an air tank with him in case he needed to breathe underwater, but he recently saw a film where the tank exploded. So, he refused to carry the tank with him in the cab of the truck. This shot was the last shot of the day and the final shot of the movie shoot. Everyone was anxious to get it over with and begin the wrap party.

On action, Vic raced the old truck down the bumpy hill. The truck was bouncing erratically as he hit the five-foot-high ramp that was built on the edge of the lake. I think the bumper hit the ramp hard on one side and knocked a hole in it. When the tire hit the hole, the truck veered straight up in the air and flipped over, hitting the water upside down. Everyone watched and prayed as the truck rapidly sunk. Time stood still as we waited breathlessly for Vic to emerge. Something went wrong. It was taking too long for him to surface. As the safety divers entered the murky water, more precious time was ticking away.

The divers came up and yelled, "We can't find him!"

The crew made a human chain and ran into the lake. The truck was in relatively shallow water not too far from the shore. The guys lifted up the rear end of the truck and dragged Vic's body out. I was holding hands with Esther Palmisano, Conrad's wife, trembling and crying.

"Don't look. Don't look, Esther," I pleaded.

I remembered my mother telling me that she had seen someone who drowned. She said she never forgot the sad image. I didn't want to see and remember Vic all swollen and blue.

The waiting ambulance raced him to the hospital with us in hot pursuit. We all sat crying and praying in the emergency room. Minutes seemed like hours. Finally, another doctor ran in and the door to the room where Vic lay attached to tubes, pumps, and machines flew open. I could not believe my eyes as I saw Vic's spirit rise out of his body. It was like an apparition floating slowly upward to the ceiling and disappearing. I was stunned and speechless. The door slammed shut and moments later the doctor came out and told us he was gone. Because Vic was under the water for so long, his passing was a blessing. I'm sure he would not have wanted to live in a vegetative state. Esther saw the same spirit rise up from Vic's body. We cried and held each other tight for a long, long time.

That day I was reminded that life is precious and can be gone in an instant. The stunts that I so loved were not all fun and games. As I drove home from the hospital that day, I was forced to reconsider whether I really wanted to continue in this dangerous career. Vic was young and had so much to live for. I believe that God has a divine plan and my only consolation during that sad confusing season was that Vic went doing what he loved doing most.

Later that night, I fell into the arms of Gary Strange—yes, that was his real name. He was a tall, extremely handsome looking man with dark wavy hair, green eyes, and a full, sexy mustache. He looked like a cross between Clark Gable and Tom Selleck. Gary was crazy about me. I had met him on the set of *Grand Theft Auto* a few months earlier. He was a "grip," the big guy on the set that pushed the camera dolly around on wheels and helped with the set and lighting as well. I was attracted to him, but I didn't want any on-location romance. That usually didn't work out, and the other stunt guys would tend to get jealous. I wanted to keep my personal dating life separate from my career.

One of the crew members had snapped a photo of Gary and I, standing under an umbrella, and sent it to me. My mother had passed down an old Polish superstition that made me believe it was bad luck to stand under an umbrella. A few weeks earlier, I had sent Gary the photo. He called me immediately and that's when we'd started dating.

I had called Gary from the hospital, frantic and distraught from the announcement of Vic's death.

He immediately said, "Please come right over, baby. I'll hold you. Everything is going to be OK."

I was in shock myself after experiencing the death of a close friend and seeing the ghostly vision of his spirit rising up from his lifeless frame.

As soon as I arrived at Gary's driveway, I was filled with a sense of foreboding. I remembered the black umbrella as I slowly drove up the dark and winding driveway to his tiny house perched on the hill. Tears streamed down my face as he opened the door, grabbed me, and held me tight. I sobbed as he took my hand and lead me to the soft black suede couch in the candlelit living room.

"Let me get you a drink," he whispered.

It seemed offering me alcohol was the only way he knew how to comfort me. He made these drinks called White Russians. They tasted like chocolate milk and consisted of vodka, Kahlúa, and cream. They were sweet and went down real easy. He handed me my drink and proceeded to pull a mirror out of the coffee table drawer. He began delicately chopping a rock of cocaine and carefully laying out two lines.

He winked at me and said, "Snort this and you'll feel better."

It was a bitter tonic for the deep sadness that I felt inside.

Gary just kept saying, "It was his time to go, it wasn't your fault."

Wishing that I had not put Vic's name in for that job, I remained uncomforted.

I'd never really been involved with drugs. I did like to smoke some pot occasionally, but I never let it interfere with the passion for my dream. This night, anything to help ease the pain and sorrow seemed like a remedy worth a try. However, the coke only masked the pain temporarily, and as the permanency of Vic's passing set in over the following days and weeks, I felt as though I'd received a devastating blow.

The day after Vic's death, I had an interview for a television commercial. When the director asked me my experience, I burst into tears and began to tell him the story of Vic's accident. Needless to say, I did not get the job.

A few days later, I had a Mass scheduled for Vic at my Catholic church, St. Mark's in Venice, California. Gary refused to go, which hurt me very much. He would not set foot in church. That should have been a huge red flag for me, but I ignored it. As the cast and crew greeted each other before the Mass, the stunt guys kept wondering aloud, "Why didn't he take an air tank with him?"

Vic's parents arrived from Pennsylvania filled with grief and sorrow. His dad looked just like him. It was uncanny. The service was unbearably sad. That my friend's life had been cut short for a movie shot seemed so pointless.

During the service, my mind wandered. Even though I knew Vic's death had been an accident, I was crushed with remorse. I knew that Vic had watched the film where the air tank blew up and he felt he had a better chance of escaping the truck after it hit the water than surviving an explosion. Little did anyone know that the truck would flip over and be a death trap for him. Instead of escaping out of the side window to freedom, he was disoriented, and although he escaped out the back window, he became trapped under the bed of the truck.

My dear friend, Father Liam Kidney, gave the Mass and it was comforting to hear his words about God's will for us. He affirmed that God had called Vic and it was all part of His divine plan. As we prayed for Vic and his family, I kept thinking of Vic's young daughter, Shelby, who would never get to know her daddy.

Vic's death changed me. For the first time in my twenty-five years on earth, I realized just how fleeting life can be. While I'd always understood at some level that my chosen career was dangerous, losing Vic made the possibility of death much more real to me. I began to wonder what the purpose of my life was meant to be.

As the days lingered on, I was drowning in a deep depression. One terrifying night, I was crying in Gary's living room and asking him why Vic's death had to happen. He had been drinking heavily and he told me to shut up. He then backhanded me and sent me flying across the living room floor. That was it. I knew I had to leave him. And leave LA too! Gathering up the few possessions that I had at his house, I made a beeline for the door. He tried to stop me, but I was fast. I escaped his reach and darted out to my Corvette. Locking the doors, starting the engine, I peeled down the driveway as he stood screaming, "Diane, Diane don't go!"

I never looked back.

8

Dream Interrupted

"Mom," I choked out through tears, "I'm coming home."

Watching a dear friend snatched from life before my eyes had me feeling unglued. I'd lost the will to pursue my dream and wanted to get back to my roots—the family and friends who knew me and loved me—so I was heading back to New Jersey. My parents worried about my well-being but were thrilled that I was coming home. They were kind and understanding and I felt their deep love.

The morning after the call, my mom, who was afraid to fly, got on the first plane out. In a heartbeat, she was at my side helping me pack and drive across the country. The world that I'd worked so hard to build had crumbled. My dream was shattered. Quietly slipping out of town, I did not say goodbye to anyone. Continuing to relive the horrible events in my head, it was the longest, most arduous drive across the country that one could imagine.

Although my mom kept telling me stories of all the fun things we could do together when we got home, nothing seemed to matter to me anymore.

When we finally arrived home, my dad held me in a long embrace.

“Everything is going to be all right, baby,” he reassured me, “I’m so glad that you are home safe.”

Unable to concentrate on anything, I sat around the house moping and staring at the television, not entirely aware of what was on. Despite my parents’ reassurance, I wasn’t at all convinced that everything was going to be all right. I had no drive, no gumption, no nothing. I was but a shell of my former self.

My mom wanted me to follow in her footsteps into the dental field and get a job as a dental assistant. *Me . . . a dental assistant? Ha!* Though the thought mortified me, I was willing to try anything just to get going again. My dream of being a successful stuntwoman was a distant memory, and I had little hope of ever amounting to anything. When I saw an ad in a local newspaper for a dental assistant, I got an interview with a middle-aged, overweight, balding dentist who had an office in the basement of his home. Immediately fond of me, he told me that he would train me and that I could start the next day. The pay was peanuts compared to what I was making in films, but it provided some semblance of normalcy. I dreaded going to the dingy basement office and doing mundane tasks like sterilizing instruments and passing tools to the doc as he called for them. Though it would be a wonderful job for many people, to me it felt like prison.

It was in the dank confines of my underground cell that relief arrived in the most unexpected packaging. One Thursday afternoon, the dentist secretly revealed to me that he always wanted to be a magician. *What? He had a dream other than inspecting and repairing teeth?* It had never occurred to me that just as I had been pining for something other than the life I was living, others might be as well. No sooner had he shared his secret dream when this rather serious, middle-aged man proceeded to step into the small closet and reappear with a black top hat on! He bowed deeply and with a grand gesture pulled a rabbit out of his top hat!

And that was the moment, in that dark dental tomb, when I returned to the land of the living.

It was time for me to get back to LA and follow my dream again. If I had thought that holding down a nine-to-five job in New Jersey would somehow make me "normal," I was learning that there was no "normal" anywhere! Working in movies and television was my passion. I needed the break I'd had while living at home, and I now had renewed enthusiasm to conquer Hollywood again. I did not want to be working in the dental office telling patients that I *used to be* a Hollywood stuntwoman. I *am* the Hollywood stuntwoman! My head and heart were leading me home to Los Angeles. And I was *ready* for round two. I was smarter, stronger, and even more dedicated. I was smarter because I realized there was only one future in mind for me. I was stronger because I took the time to rest and revitalize my body and soul. There was no denying the call I felt and no stopping me. Conquering the fear of death that was a strong possibility in doing stunts, combined with my renewed laser focus of following my dream, propelled me to plan my return trip to Los Angeles.

Even my parents could see that I was unsatisfied with the mundane existence that my life had become. Though they loved having me at home, they supported my decision to return to Hollywood and take another stab at my California dream.

When I'd set off for California with Dave the first time, starry eyed and hopeful, it seemed like the world was my oyster. I could only see success.

As we pursue our dreams, we may face obstacles we could never have seen coming. For me, it was Vic's death. Losing him knocked the wind out of my sails. (Thankfully, one New Jersey rabbit blew fresh air back into them!) Maybe the obstacle you faced was a financial failure. Perhaps you lost a job you loved. Or your dream may have been derailed by countless other obstacles outside of your control—or even *within* your control. As you set your sights on the dream in your heart, expect to face challenges, disappointments, and disruptions. While they may slow you down for a minute, they don't have to signal the death of your dream. You can move beyond the obstacle to take the next step in your journey.

Sights set once again on Hollywood, I called up good old Dave in Miami.

"Hey Dave," I announced, "I'm ready to go back to LA. Wanna drive across the country with me again?"

"Sure doll," he agreed. "When do you want to leave?"

We left for Los Angeles the following week. My parents helped me pack the car once again for the long journey. My mom was crying as we left, and my dad was cheering me on.

"Go get 'em baby," he whispered in my ear as he squeezed me tight.

This time our drive across the country was direct. No sightseeing, no joyriding. I was on a mission to get back to Los Angeles and start working again. It had been six long months since I packed up my dreams and went home, and I was ready for action.

Living back in Marina Del Rey, I began working as a cocktail waitress in a little Italian restaurant to tide me over until movie work came my way.

That's where I met Sean.

Sean was strikingly handsome, tan, with dark, perfectly coifed hair, hazel eyes, and a killer smile. He was dressed in a buttery dark-brown leather jacket and was sitting alone at the bar. Our eyes met and there was an immediate attraction. The owner of the restaurant introduced us, and we made plans for our first date. Sean asked me to go to brunch on Sunday. I told him that I went to Mass at St. Mark's Catholic Church and asked him if he would like to go with me. He declined and said that he would meet me after Mass at Friday's restaurant. Another guy with no church. *Possible red flag,* I thought. But our brunch date was an enormous success. We talked for hours and had a lot in common. I laughed the entire time and felt a strong connection. I looked forward to seeing him again.

Meanwhile, I was busy sending out pictures and résumés to agents, all my stunt contacts, and anyone who I could think of to get me more film work. Waiting on tables was getting old extremely fast.

When I called Bill Lane, he said that he was about to start a new television show called *The Misadventures of Sheriff Lobo* starring Claude Akins. He thought I would make a great double for Tara Buckman, a bubbly young blond who could have passed for my sister. Bill informed me that I needed to get on Teddy's answering service so that I would have a pager. Long before smartphones made most of us *constantly* accessible, Teddy's was the famed answering service for all the top stunt coordinators, stuntmen, stuntwomen, and directors. I told Bill that I tried to get on Teddy's, and they told me they had a waiting list of two hundred people and that I could not get on for years. With one phone call, Bill got me on the service. After his intervention, I began to hear more "Yes ma'am" instead of "Diane *who*?" I secretly felt that I had really made it by just getting on Teddy's and having my very own pager!

Thrilled to be working regularly on a television series, I was back in the saddle again and lovin' it. *The Misadventures of Sheriff Lobo* starred Claude Akins as Sheriff Lobo. He was a giant, sweet, always-smiling, willing-to-lend-a-hand kind of guy. Each day on *Sheriff Lobo* there was always something different: car chases, fights, falls, roller skating. I did it all. My dream was back in focus. My life was getting back on track.

As a stunt double for Tara Buckman—who was blond, about five feet, five inches tall, and weighed about 115 pounds, was just like me—I worked a couple days a week. Because Tara wasn't very athletic, I got to do many simple stunts like fights and pratfalls. I also got to do car chases (my favorite), motorcycle riding, horseback riding, and whatever was needed.

The rumor on the set was that Hal Needham, a famous stuntman for Burt Reynolds and a legend in his time, had brought Tara to Hollywood, bought her new boobs, and gotten her a role on *Sheriff Lobo*. Hal had been a second unit director while shooting the movie *Cannonball Run* in South Carolina, where he met Tara, a pretty waitress at the local hangout. He promised he'd make her a star and he'd made good on his word.

The stunt guys—largely responsible for keeping the rumors about Tara's opportunity in Hollywood alive—joked about gathering a pool of money and buying me a big set of boobs, but that is where I drew the line. I liked my boobs as they were and thought they were the perfect size for me. I could always use padded pushups! The fact is that I was normally proportioned and really didn't care about having huge mammary glands.

This said, of course appearance mattered a great deal on the set. The hairdressers tried to talk stunt doubles into cutting and dyeing our hair to match the person we'd be doubling, especially if working on a series. I liked my hair just the way it was, so I never complained about wearing the wigs. The hair people, however, complained because they said viewers could tell that it was a wig. My theory was that if you could tell that it was a wig, then you could also tell that it wasn't the actress as well. Sometimes the hairdressers would slam the bobby pins into the stunt double's scalp extra hard because they were upset that they had to wig us all the time. And God forbid if the wig came off during a stunt. That happened a few times and it made the hairdresser look really bad.

Whenever I was needed on set, Bill would beep me on my pager. I only used the pager for work, so I knew when I heard the glorious beep, a job was waiting. It was music to my ears whenever the beeper went off! The moment I heard its beautiful chirp, I would immediately look for a phone booth to call in to see when and where I was needed. I kept a huge bag of change with me so that I was ready to feed the pay phone ASAP to get my next assignment.

One day I was at the horse races at Hollywood Park when my pager went off. To my horror, there were no phone booths at the track! I suppose it had something to do with betting and the bookies. I immediately left the track to search for the familiar public phone booth available at many intersections. It was necessary to be quick with the return call because if you were not available, they would hire someone else. Usually, the call was for a job the very next day.

Compared to what I'd made as a dental assistant and cocktail waitress, the pay was terrific! I worked either a daily contract of approximately $400 a day or a weekly contract of approximately $1,600 a week. At the time, it was a lot of money to be paid for doing the job that I loved. The studio that produced *Sheriff Lobo*,

Universal, liked to keep me on a weekly contract to ensure my availability. Other stunt coordinators were calling me for other jobs on *Charlie's Angels*, *Fall Guy*, and various movies. I tried always to be available for *Sheriff Lobo* because it was a steady job, and the residuals would be pouring in after the show went on reruns. Plus, I trusted Bill Lane and enjoyed working with him. He knew his trade, was safe, and was a real gentleman. As for the residuals, when the first primetime rerun aired, I would get paid nearly the amount that I made when filming the stunt the first time. However, the money declined with subsequent showings after that. Going to the mailbox became a joyous occasion when I'd find huge residual checks that helped feather my nest. I still get residual checks for *Kojak*; *Charlie's Angels*; *MacGyver*; *Walker, Texas Ranger*; *Annie Hall*; *Titanic*; and a myriad of other television shows and movies that I worked on many moons ago.

In addition to the daily or weekly rate, I would get a stunt adjustment, or additional money, to do the actual stunt. Depending on the degree of difficulty of the stunt, the dollar amount would increase. For instance, if I had to jump off a twenty-foot building, I might ask the stunt coordinator for $500 more than the daily or weekly rate that I was being paid. The additional $500 would be for one time, and if the director wanted a second take, it would be an additional $500 unless I screwed up the first take. If it was my error, I would do the next shot pro bono. Usually, the stunt coordinator would give you what you asked for unless he was on a tight budget. Then he would say, "Would you do it for $300 and I'll make it up to you on the next one?" Of course I would agree, otherwise I'd never work for that guy again. Some coordinators didn't even ask for a rate, they just doled out a number at the end of the day. In some cases, a stunt double would get nothing extra. We'd choose to live with it because we were grateful to have a day's work. Ideally, we would get some residuals down the road. All the jobs added to my pension income eventually as well. There were also overtime and meal penalties, which could really boost the amount of your check. If a stuntperson was not fed within six hours of arriving on the set, the production would incur penalties for each and every fifteen-minute interval, which quickly added up. Thankfully, there was always a craft services table with lots of goodies so cast and crew would never starve to death while waiting for the actual meal to be served. No one really cared whether the meal was late because we were happy to get the extra money on our check from the meal penalties. The Screen Actors Guild, the union that monitors these benefits, really protects stuntpeople and actors in many ways. As a SAG member, I'd go to the mailbox, see the Screen Actors Guild envelope, and not know whether the check inside would add up to lunch money or something much bigger. SAG keeps a tight eye on the residuals because guild dues are based on the entire amount of money members make. Not only was I blessed with joy in my work and a zest to follow my dream of being a top Hollywood stuntwoman, I was being paid handsomely for the job I'd always loved doing.

Before Vic's death, I had fallen off the "horse" before. While performing stunts, I'd had my fair share of scrapes, bruises, and injuries, just like my colleagues. And I'd always dusted myself off and kept going. After losing Vic, though, I didn't want to get back on the horse. I needed a season of rest and healing. But when a New Jersey dentist pulled a rabbit out of his top hat, I knew I had a choice. I could have chosen the steady paycheck, or I could get back on the horse. Never once have I regretted returning to Hollywood and climbing back up on that—admittedly dangerous—horse!

Maybe your dream has been deferred because you fell off the horse. You paused to care for a loved one. You couldn't afford tuition. You faced another unanticipated obstacle. Sometimes, the best thing to do is to hop right back on. But other times you may benefit from a season of rest and healing. If your dream has stalled, notice what you need right now and make sure you practice self-care by accessing what you need to thrive again.

As I was returning to work, Sean and I were falling in love. He was a terrific dancer—in the *Saturday Night Fever* style—and we danced and dined in all the hot spots in LA. Plus he looked like a dark-haired version of a Ken doll. Sean was a regional manager for a company. Not an exciting job, but I really didn't care about what he did for a living. All I knew is that we had a magical time together drinking and partying. Sean asked me to marry him after only two months of dating, but I was unsure. Despite the thrill of the whirlwind romance, my instinct kept begging me to take it slow.

Whenever he'd bring up the idea, I'd say, "It's too soon, ask me another time."

As time went on, Sean grew on me. I thought about the cute kids we might have one day. I was approaching twenty-nine and practically all my friends were married. I didn't want to turn thirty and not be married. Even though I still had some reservations about Sean, I looked forward to the next time he would ask me to marry him. After waiting four more months, Sean asked me again, and I said yes. Unfortunately, just around the same time he asked me to marry him, Sean got fired from his job. A red flag I couldn't have seen coming.

Not long after our engagement, I got a call from my acting agent to fly to Georgia to play Keith Carradine's girlfriend in the film *The Long Riders*. Though I was thrilled, Sean wasn't pleased. Tension was growing in our relationship, and I suspected that he resented my success. But I was in love with him, and love is blind and stupid most of the time.

I flew to Georgia, and the next day I met the director, Walter

Hill. On a hot, steamy day in Georgia, Walter explained to me that I would be playing a Swedish hooker, and Keith was spending his last night with me in the brothel before the big shoot-out in the morning. I will just say that the Georgia heat was nothing compared to the steamy, pretend love scene between the sheets. I had one line to say: *Ge mig en kyss*. Which means, "Give me a kiss" in Swedish. My Swedish accent left a lot to be desired. As we tumbled around hot and sweaty on camera, I thought about adding a stunt to our scene by falling out of bed. Ultimately, I decided that I had better stick to the director's wishes. As I returned to LA, I was sure that this film, a big budget movie with a well-known director, was going to be my big breakout in the film business. Even though I wasn't doing stunts in the film, the visibility could certainly lead to more stunt jobs.

About a week before the film was scheduled to open, I received a letter from Walter Hill saying that he was sorry but there wasn't enough screen time to include my scene in the movie. I was left on the cutting room floor! It was so nice of him to let me know, but still I was devastated. The day the picture opened, I walked by a theater in Westwood where it was showing and, to my astonishment, there was a still shot of me and Keith in bed in the kiosk window. Hopeful, I thought maybe they changed their mind, and I was still in the film. I eagerly bought a ticket and ran inside. As the film reached the end before the big shoot-out, I waited for my scene. But there was nothing but a shot of the brothel in the background and all the girls standing on the porch. I was disappointed and angry. *How could they use false advertising with my picture outside the theater to draw people in?* When I called the studio and complained, my shot was removed from the ad campaign. That's Hollywood!

The agony of landing on the cutting room floor eventually dissipated, but it was always extremely disappointing to disappear from the final cut of the movie. Plus, most everyone who knew

I had worked on the movie would say, "I saw that movie and I didn't see you in it."

I'd just laugh and say, "Check the cutting room floor!"

9

Ignoring the Voice Inside

"We have to talk," Sean said with a serious expression.

We were walking to the travel agent in Century City to book our honeymoon trip when he stopped me beside a low stone wall to have this difficult conversion.

Hearing those words is never, ever good.

I sat up on the wall and asked, "What's up?"

He answered, "I have no money, and I think we should postpone the wedding."

Unfazed, I said, "It's now or never. My parents put deposits on the reception venue, the band, the flowers, the photographer, and my dress is ordered. Nice time to tell me that you are broke."

As I received Sean's words, another old Polish superstition that my mother had taught me rang loudly in my head, "To postpone means bad luck." I couldn't bear to tell my parents that we were postponing the wedding. The invitations had been sent and the beautiful Catholic church in my hometown was booked. My favorite priest, Father J. Patrick Kelly, had agreed to do the ceremony.

"Don't worry," I assured Sean, "we'll get plenty of cash for wedding gifts, and we can use that to pay for the honeymoon."

In many New Jersey weddings, the bride traditionally has a pretty white satin cash bag, and at the end of the evening, the guests file by and give a card with cash as a wedding gift. Reluctantly, Sean agreed to proceed. Longing to be married, I chose to ignore all the signs that postponing, or canceling altogether, would have been most prudent.

It rained on our wedding day. Per Polish superstition, it was yet another ominous sign. The limousine driver was late, too. Another bad omen. The wedding was a traditional Catholic ceremony with Mass and communion, and the church was decorated in incredible white roses. In my elegant white gown, I looked and felt like a fairy-tale princess.

It was pouring rain as we climbed up the long staircase together to enter St. Leo's Church.

I complained, "Dad, you are stepping on my train."

Jovial, he explained, "I don't want to get my feet wet!"

We laughed all the way into church. The ceremony was very moving, and I was elated when Father Jim pronounced us husband and wife and we walked up the aisle hand in hand. The reception was a big party with great food and the fabulous band I had chosen. The next morning, Sean and I left bright and early for our honeymoon in romantic Maui.

After our trip, when we returned to our new apartment in Marina Del Rey, I was forced to see the reality I was facing. I hadn't lived with Sean before the wedding and hadn't known the details of his finances. But as I flipped through the mail, I was horrified at all the credit card debt that this guy was in. Every card was maxed out to the limit, and there were countless cards. I, who paid all my credit card charges in full every month so I wouldn't incur interest payments, couldn't believe what I'd married into. I had savings, no debt, and I was making big money in my career. Who knew that all the dinners and social activities that we'd been enjoying were being charged and only minimum payments were being paid? That was when I decided to keep our finances separate. As a result, Sean scrambled for a job and finally got a job as a restaurant manager at El Torito in Marina Del Rey. He worked many nights and weekends.

I was not a happy newlywed.

My work, though, was better than ever. I was doubling Cheryl Ladd on *Charlie's Angels* and Heather Thomas on *Fall Guy*, besides working other television shows and films.

The first Christmas Sean and I shared as mister and missus, he let me know at the last minute that he couldn't go to New Jersey, as we'd planned, because the other manager at work, Bob, was in the hospital. Because Christmas was always so special in our home, I was deeply upset. I'd so wanted our first Christmas as husband and wife to be one to remember.

When I arrived in New Jersey, my dad could tell I was upset.

On a whim my dad, who clearly didn't trust Sean, said, "Why don't you call the restaurant and ask for Bob?"

When I called the restaurant and asked for Bob, he answered the phone.

"Sean told me that you were in the hospital!" I exclaimed, in shock.

There was dead silence.

Sean got on the next plane to New Jersey, but things were different between us. Having caught him in a big lie, I no longer trusted him. Being fired from his job a few months later didn't help our relationship either.

Though we looked like the perfect beautiful couple, underneath deep trouble was brewing. When I insisted on marriage counseling, Sean confessed to the therapist that he was resentful that I was living my dream while he had to do a job that he hated. I was surprised to hear him say that he had a dream to own his own restaurant. I also had another dream: I really wanted a baby. But the apartment complex we lived in did not allow kids, and so we needed to get a house first, as well as shovel him out of debt.

Because I wanted Sean to follow his dream, we found a location for him to open Club Café, a restaurant of his own, inside a tennis and health club in Culver City. There was a pool, a gym, and lots of members. I financed the restaurant along with my dad's help. Maybe the Club Café would help him realize his dream and strengthen our marriage.

A few days before the restaurant was scheduled to open, I went out to hustle with my tall, red-headed friend Mary Peters. "Hustle" is a term that meant "looking for work." Mary and I were quite different physically with our height, weight, and hair color, so there was no competition between us for jobs. Plus, I was known for my top-notch driving skills, which was another factor that set us apart. Mary and I always had a fabulous time sneaking onto the lots at Paramount, 20th Century Fox, MGM, and the Burbank studios. Sometimes we tried to blend in with the employees coming to work in the morning or returning from lunch walking past the guards at the security check point.

"Just look like you belong," I'd urge Mary, "and keep walking fast with the crowd."

Sometimes I'd strike up conversation with a stranger who worked there, just to blend in with the returning employees. At a few of the gates, we got to know the guards. Eventually, after sweet-talking them, they'd let us on the lot. Our youth and beauty allowed us to get away with a lot.

One day when I was feeling particularly bold, I drove past the guard without stopping. I just waved. My plan backfired when he immediately sent security after us and they kicked us off the lot. For us it was an amusing game.

When we *did* make it onto the lot, we would go to the hair and makeup department and examine the list of movies and television shows that were shooting on the lot that day. We knew most of the hairdressers and makeup folks from working on shows, and they were always happy to see us and let us look at the lists. If there was a stunt coordinator on the list, we would make our way to the soundstage or set on the backlot. If we didn't know the coordinator, we would ask a few people to point him out. Usually, filming was going on and we would patiently wait for a break in the shoot. When we saw our opening, we'd approach the person we hoped would become our future boss with a picture and résumé in hand.

On one particularly hot, muggy summer day in the valley, I saw Ronnie Rondell standing in the corner of the soundstage. Ronnie was a famous stuntman who ran a lot of jobs. Short and stocky, he had a complexion that resembled old, tanned leather. Nervously, I approached him with my photo and résumé in hand.

As I was creeping up on him, Mary shouted, "Ronnie, you need to meet my buddy, Diane Peterson."

Thank God, she knows him.

Mary gave him a big hug as he was smiling and checking me out.

Extending my hand, I said, "Ronnie, I'm so glad to meet you, I've heard so much about you. I'd really love to work with you sometime."

Glancing at my photo and résumé, Ronnie grabbed some cookies from the craft service table and said, "Thanks for coming by ladies, I'll call you if something turns up."

After we left the lot, Mary and I went to a local hangout called Residuals. It was a dark, seedy bar that offered a free drink to anyone who brought in a residual check, or "royalties," for under five dollars. They would take your check and pin it on the wall alongside thousands of checks plastering the walls. A lot of stunt guys hung out there, so it was an extra good place to celebrate our successful hustle day.

We were having a drink and laughing about our day when my pager buzzed. I ran to the pay phone and called Teddy's. The operator said Ronnie Rondell had called for my availability for the following day.

I quickly said, "I'm available! What is the stunt?"

The operator didn't know but assured me that she would call me later with the details of the stunt, location, and my call time.

I ran back to Mary and screamed, "I'm working for Ronnie Rondell tomorrow!"

Happy for me, Mary hugged me as we said our goodbyes, and I drove singing and smiling all the way home. I didn't know what

I would be doing, but I was confident that I could handle anything. Once again, my dream was coming true.

Later that night, Teddy's called me to give me the location and my call time. Still having no idea who I was doubling or what I was doing, I packed my Red Bag of Courage into my little orange corvette and went to bed early. In addition to all of my stunt pads, that beloved red bag included my Blessed Saint Christopher medal, hanging by a safety pin on the inside pocket for good measure.

Scheduled to be on the set at 6:00 a.m., I awoke early, well before my alarm. My mental clock was finely tuned. Hopping into the Vette, I headed out in the cloak of darkness. Around daybreak, I arrived at the location, which was an old convent in the Pasadena area. I immediately felt a sense of calm and safety in that holy place. When I checked in with the AD (assistant director), he escorted me to my dressing room. After dropping off my bag, eager to find out who I was doubling and what stunt I'd been hired to do, I ventured out to find Ronnie Rondell.

Before I found Ronnie, I learned that the show was called *Massarati and the Brain*, and that it was a pilot for a television series. The actress was a no-name, someone I had never heard of. I finally tracked down Ronnie at the back of the convent. Surrounded by the director and a slew of cameramen and grips, he was setting up a large stunt crash pad approximately ten feet by ten feet in a driveway and was looking up at a window high above an awning on the side of the convent.

"Good morning, Ronnie," I greeted him.

Focused, Ronnie pointed at the window, which was about twenty feet up, and said, "You are going to bust through that window and land here. Then you are going to get up and run. A helicopter will swoop down as you jump up, grab the skid, and take off."

Yikes, is that all? I thought to myself.

Once again feeling my fear of heights, my mother's words echoed in my head, "Don't go near the edge."

I smiled at Ronnie and said, "No problem."

As I was walking away, he added, "Oh, by the way, I want you to come feet first when you hit the bag. I want it to look like you are jumping. And don't hit the middle of the bag because you may bounce back and hit your head on the air conditioner unit."

As I smiled and nodded, I heard Alex, who I'd first met in New York, preaching, "Don't ever go feet first, kick out and land on your back."

But this was Ronnie Rondell, and I had to do it his way or I thought that I would never work for him again. Knowing I'd be increasing the risk of injury, the what-ifs raced through my mind as I headed to the hair and makeup trailer. There I saw a photo of the woman who I was doubling. She had dark hair and was noticeably smaller than I was. I wondered why he chose me for this rather big stunt and why he didn't explain to me what the job entailed before bringing me in. After the hairdresser secured the hideous brown wig on my head with extra pins and slapped some red lipstick on me, I headed to the set.

On the way there, I stopped in the convent's tiny, dimly lit chapel. Candles glowed and wax dripped onto the cold, dark tile. I lit a candle and kneeled down to pray.

"God, please keep me safe and give me courage."

With renewed strength, I climbed the winding staircase to the upper room where I was greeted by a pack of eight vicious-looking Doberman pinschers who stared at me as if I was their next meal. Ronnie forgot to tell me that the vicious Dobermans would be chasing me. Although the dog trainer assured me that the dogs would obey him, I didn't trust him for a second. I heard the murmur of a low growl as I sneaked past my vicious pursuers. Peering out the large glass six-foot-by-six-foot window, I gazed at the awning jutting out under it. I knew I had to clear this awning in order to land on my target, which I could barely see.

"Don't worry, you can do this," I kept telling myself.

Then I could hear Alex in my head: "Don't go feet first into anything."

Ronnie came up to ask me if I was ready and to remind me to come feet first. He explained that he wanted it to look like the other stuntman on the ground was catching me.

"OK," I agreed, but I did not feel right about it.

I also wondered if I would bang heads with the stuntman on the ground.

I was in a real predicament.

My head was saying "Don't do it," but I knew I would look like a coward if I didn't do it. Word would get out about how I froze and chickened out at the last minute. The filming would be severely delayed until they could get another stuntwoman to arrive and do the job. No, I had to go for it. This was Ronnie Rondell, and I had to do a great job.

I heard the director yell, "Camera's rolling."

The vicious Dobermans, their sharp teeth ready to devour me, strained on their choke collars.

The director announced, "Action, Diane."

Racing toward the giant glass window, blood pressure rising, the dogs nipped at my heels. My heart pounded as I hit the window. I knew something was off.

That was too hard. Too fast.

CRASH! the glass shattered.

Oh my God, I'm going to miss the bag.

I fell for what felt like an eternity.

WHACK!

Hitting the corner of the bag, my foot slid off with mighty force and smashed into the driveway. Excruciating pain shot through my entire body, and I thought that my back was broken. In two seconds, my heel and ankle swelled up like a tree trunk. I could hear the helicopter coming, but I couldn't move.

I heard the director yell, "Cut!"

The medic ran in, and the ambulance screeched up. I was crying so hard and in so much pain.

Why didn't I listen to myself? Why didn't I do it my way?

10

Paying Attention

The ride to the hospital felt endless. I was in agony. Every bump in the road sent thousands of pain waves coursing through my body. I felt like screaming, but I was in shock and nothing would come out of my parched mouth. I was rushed into the busy hospital emergency room. Everyone was asking me what happened, and all I could utter was that I jumped through a window. The nurses looked at me like I belonged in the psych ward. I was too weak, dizzy, and in pain to explain more. I lay in the bright, cold, hallway of the antiseptic-smelling hospital, sick to my stomach from the intense pain. All the emergency rooms were full of other patients, so I lay in the hallway begging for pain medication. The mean old nurses said that I had to wait for the orthopedic surgeon to arrive before they could give me anything to ease my agony. I thought I would go insane from the pain. I wept uncontrollably and wondered why this had happened to me?

Why didn't I listen to that little voice in my head, "Don't go feet first, don't go feet first, no matter what."

Certain my career was over, I just knew I might never walk again.

God, Please, God let this pain go away.

I prayed feverishly as the uncaring nurses wheeled me into the X-ray room.

As they tried to position my enormously swollen heel and ankle joint for the X-rays, I screamed bloody murder.

"Please, I need some pain meds now," I cried.

"Relax," they barked, "the doctor will be here soon."

I so wished that I could turn back the hands of time.

When they shoved my gurney back into the frigid hallway, I spotted my husband Sean. I was still shaking and crying when he got to me.

"What did you do to yourself now?" he demanded. "You really fucked up this time, didn't you?"

My excruciating pain and career-ending injuries were clearly an inconvenience to him.

"The restaurant is opening in two days," he complained, "You couldn't have picked better time to get hurt."

I could hardly believe my ears. Instead of holding and comforting me, all he could do was worry about how this accident would impact my ability to help him open the restaurant.

At that moment the fat, red-faced, bald doctor showed up. I guess this emergency call disturbed his evening because he gruffly said, "I looked at your X-rays, and you are going to need pins to hold your heel together. You will never walk normally again. You shattered your heelbone in five places. I need to operate now."

Aside from the terrifying prognosis, I got an unbelievably bad feeling from him and did not like his bedside manner one bit. I was not going to let him touch me.

"No thanks, Doc, I'm getting a second opinion," I blurted out.

His face revealed that my refusal had angered him.

Just then, my friend Mary showed up. Bad news travels fast, and she'd gotten word that I'd been injured.

Mary coaxed, "Diane, listen to me. You must get Dr. Rosenfeld to help you. He fixes all the stunt guys and is the doctor for the Raiders. I'll call him now."

Mary called Dr. Rosenfeld and he got on the phone with me.

"Don't worry, Diane, I'll take excellent care of you. I'll be waiting for you at Cedars Sinai Hospital in Beverly Hills."

I immediately felt safe, and I knew that I was making the right choice.

As I was rushed back into the ambulance, the creepy old doctor who'd delivered the grim news refused to give me any pain medication for the ride. Once again, I had to endure the long journey in excruciating pain. Pasadena to Beverly Hills took forever, and every bump in the road felt like a thousand daggers in my heel. My entire foot felt like it was going to explode by the time we arrived at Cedars.

Dr. Rosenfeld was waiting there, smiling, and said, "You don't have to be in pain anymore, Diane. I'll take good care of you."

He then calmly added, "I looked at your X-rays, my dear, and I'm going to do a closed reduction and put a cast on. No pins for you.

It will be far better in the long run. You will be able to walk and run without limping. Please, don't worry."

Within minutes I was feeling no pain after the much-needed shot. I felt confident I was in good hands with Dr. Rosenfeld. He was a sports orthopedic surgeon and knew exactly what the best surgery and treatment would be for my heel and my future.

Will I even have a career after this? What will I do next?

It seemed my dream was being shattered along with my heel.

Dr. Rosenfeld, who couldn't operate until the swelling subsided, explained that my heel and leg would have to be elevated and packed in ice for approximately one week because of the enormous swelling. I was wheeled to my private room where I cried for hours. But not because of the pain. There was no pain since I'd received the medication. I wept because recalling the broken leg I'd suffered as a teenager, and the months of rehab, I understood how long my recovery was going to take. I worried about my future, my marriage, and my life with no dream to sustain me.

"Stuntman killed in high fall jump."

As I lay in the hospital bed watching the news, I saw those six awful words emblazoned on the screen. Turning up the volume, I learned that it was Jack Tyree with whom I worked on several films. He was doing an eighty-foot-high fall from a cliff for the film *The Sword and the Sorcerer*, when a part of the cliff gave way as he pushed off and fell short of the airbag. Praying for Jack, a sweet, kind, loving man, I also thanked God that my injuries were not worse. At that time, I'd known three stuntmen who'd had been killed. *Is this career worth losing my life?*

No.

One week later when I awoke from the operation, I thought my big toe was going to explode. I screamed for the nurse and, miraculously, Dr. Rosenfeld arrived with a tiny saw and immediately split the cast open. My leg had swollen up so much again that the pain was unbearable. He quickly remedied that with a shot of "feel good." Whatever was in those shots made me feel like I didn't have a care in the world. Dr. Rosenfeld told me that I would be in a cast for about ten weeks, which sounded like a lifetime to me. He said that I would need to come to his office in Beverly Hills once a week for a checkup. The one light in the very dark tunnel that was my future was that I'd injured my left foot and I would be able to drive. I hated the crutches. Every time I put my leg down from an elevated position to try to maneuver on those hideous sticks, major pain and pressure would torpedo into my heel as blood raced to the injured area.

My dream of thriving as a stuntwoman was now all but a distant memory. So, as I hung out on the couch at home, I focused on my brother John's upcoming wedding in Vermont. Johnny and I were always super close growing up. He was twenty-one months older than me and a fabulous big brother. He was an excellent osteopathic doctor as well. I was invited to be a bridesmaid and had agreed before my accident. I worried about how I would be able to make it to Vermont in my cast-ridden condition. How could I walk down the aisle on those hideous crutches? I was so embarrassed by them. I knew that I could not and would not disappoint my dear brother. Dr. Rosenfeld had assured me that I would be able to fly to Vermont, though he also explained that the altitude would make me quite uncomfortable in the cast. The pressure inside the cast would be extreme, but the little blue pills would keep me in bliss land until I landed. I felt so relieved knowing that I could be there for my brother whom I loved so much.

The opening of the Club Café that my husband and I had been working on had been scheduled for the day after I got out of the hospital. I was distraught that I could be of no help. My husband was particularly disgusted that all I could do was sit with my leg elevated and only supervise what would be going on at the restaurant opening.

I decided that it would be far better for me to stay home and hobble out to the deck in the marina near our apartment with a few little blue pills in hand and a plastic cup of white wine. Perhaps the tension that I felt with him, and the lingering image of his unkindness, would evaporate into the ocean breeze. I would spend my time reading, making friends with the birds, and waving to the boats passing by.

The weeks dragged on endlessly. It was a sad state of affairs when the highlight of my week was going to see Dr. Rosenfeld in Beverly Hills for my follow up visits and X-rays. He always flirted with me, though, and made me laugh. He wore an enormous Super Bowl ring and joked that if I married him, I could have it. He reminded me to be confident in the fact that I would soon be walking around normally and enjoying life again.

Finally, the day came when he was to remove the cast. When Dr. Rosenfeld sawed the cast in half and gently pulled my leg out, I cried and cried when I saw my skinny, white, hairy leg. My ankle and heel were still swollen after ten long weeks of being trapped in the hard-shell cast, and I really thought I was maimed forever. I could barely step down on my foot without feeling like I was going to pass out. Dr. Rosenfeld assured me that after six to eight weeks of physical therapy, three times a week, I would be walking like a gorgeous runway model again. I had my serious doubts at that point, but I chose to believe in him and myself. I was determined to do all that I could possibly do to be back to normal as soon as possible. I knew the new normal would always be altered by my injury, but the extent of the change was unknown and to be determined.

Physical therapy was grueling. There was stretching and pulling and endless circles made with my tender ankle and heel. Hot wax baths were followed by ice-cold plunges in stainless steel vats up to my knee. My physical therapist, Joanna Guthrie, was amazing. She massaged my ankle, heel, and calf and always made me feel so much better despite the agony that I was going through. She helped my recovery so very much with her healing hands and loving spirit.

Though I wasn't thrilled about the duration and pain involved in the healing process, I knew that the outcome could have been so much worse. Had I bowed to the advice of the angry red-faced doctor in the emergency room, pins would have been holding my heel together, and I never would have walked normally again. That very morning I'd silenced the voice inside cautioning me against doing the stunt the way I'd been instructed, and it had cost me dearly. And yet somehow, in the hospital, while in excruciating pain, I'd had the courage to listen to the inner voice warning me not to trust the angry doctor. And my instinct was rewarded when Mary showed up and made the call to Dr. Rosenfeld.

Very few of us were raised to trust our inner voice. Our parents may have encouraged us to practice wisdom, to seek advice, to use sound judgment, but they might not have ever guided us to pay attention to what our deep insides knew to be true and right. This was one lesson I was learning the hard way! But you can bet that I haven't forgotten it. Since that fateful day, I've chosen to listen to that inner voice and let it help guide my decisions. That doesn't mean that whim or instinct are the boss of me, but it does mean that I no longer silence that inner voice that is gently offering me information, instinct, or insight I need to consider.

After the months of prescribed therapy, every time I stepped down on my foot with all my weight, it felt like someone was stabbing me with an ice pick, deep inside the joint.

Dr. Rosenfeld said that I had two choices. The first was that he could do a fusion with some bone material from my hip and cement the ankle joint and heel together. This would eliminate the pain, but I would never be able to wear high heels or ski or do many of the sports activities that I loved. Plus, I would walk with a limp for the rest of my life. The second option was that he could cut open the heel area and shave the heel bone down, thus relieving pressure on the nerves. He explained to me that when the five pieces of the heel grew back together, the mass had been too big for the joint, and the nerves were getting crushed and pinched when I attempted to walk. He warned me that there was a chance that this operation might not be successful, and if so, then I would need the fusion after all. The healing time would be another twelve weeks.

I needed time to think and weigh my options.

Because I couldn't resign myself to not being able to wear high heels, walk normally, or ski ever again, I decided, after much agonizing, that I would opt for the experimental choice B: shaving the heelbone down. And I knew that if the operation wasn't successful, I would have an additional ten to twelve more weeks after the fusion.

After the first surgery, Dr. Rosenfeld had told me that I'd needed a lot of anesthesia to keep me under. I was afraid that this time they would give me too much and I would never wake up. At thirty-two, I worried my career was over, and now I feared for my life. But a life without being able to do the things that I loved to do was no life at all. Without a dream to pursue, I couldn't visualize a future. Though I was really scared, I knew the decision I made was my best option.

I woke up from the surgery to find Dr. Rosenfeld smiling at me. He reported that the procedure went well, and we would just have to wait and see. Three more months in the cast seemed like another eternity.

Daily, I'd hobble to the restaurant on my crutches and sit behind the bar making drinks for the customers. My Playboy Bunny training enabled me to be an excellent bartender. At least I could contribute to the family business in some way. Plus, I received disability insurance money, and at the time, the Screen Actors Guild would match a member's disability check with another one of an equal amount. So even though I was not working, I was pulling in some good money.

When the cast was removed, I once again had to endure three more months of therapy. But this time I could feel the difference in my ability to move almost immediately. Joanna was happy to see my progress, and I was thrilled to have renewed enthusiasm. Day by day I was getting stronger, and my gait was rapidly improving. Dr. Rosenfeld told the insurance company that I could never do stunts again due to the risk of getting reinjured. Did I really want to continue in such a dangerous field?

The insurance company sent me to do a series of career aptitude assessments to determine what other interests I had. Television and film kept showing up as my passion and strength. My creative mind and sense of adventure were evident. So, the insurance company agreed to send me to a film school for a year to study production in all aspects.

I immersed myself in studies and practical workshops at the Los Angeles Television and Film school. While I enjoyed everything I was learning, working as a stuntwoman was never far from my mind. I desperately missed the thrill, the excitement, the adrenaline rush. I just could not see myself content with directing or being a cameraperson.

I kept thinking, *Will I ever do another stunt? Can I? Do I have the nerve to tempt fate another time? Can I find the courage to overcome my fears?* But I knew that I could not go through the agony that I just experienced another time.

Maybe next time it would be worse.

11

Beeper Panic

Bebeep, Bebeep Bebeep!

I hadn't heard the sound of a pager beep in eighteen months when mine suddenly beeped. I'd been scouring the trade papers looking for work on the production end of the business and had even had one interview with a producer at Universal, but nothing came of it. I was anxious to start working in some capacity in the business when I heard the once-familiar chime.

It meant only one thing: I was being summoned for stunt work.

My heart raced as I envisioned shattering bones, ambulance sirens, and flashbacks of intense pain. *What should I do? Ignore the beep? Or face my future?*

My hand shook as I reached for the phone.

Have I lost my nerve? "I don't have to do this," I reminded myself.

Or did I?

When the old stunt guys had visited me in the hospital they'd said, "You have to get hurt once, girl, to be good—so you will never do that again." Was I rugged like they were, bouncing back after a serious injury? Their passion for what they loved was infectious. I wasn't sure I was ready to hang up the Red Bag of Courage.

But now, for the first time I, who was once so fearless, doubted myself. Could I muster up the courage to walk onto another set as the Hollywood stuntwoman?

Go for it!

I heard the voice inside clearly.

Knowing it was the right thing to do, I called Teddy's.

The cheerful voice at Teddy's answering service said, "Oh, hi Diane, we've missed you. How's your heel doing? Ready for work?"

I took a deep breath and tried to be brave.

"Thanks, yes, it's good to be back. My heel is all healed! Thank God! Who is calling me for work?"

I was sincerely hoping it was not going to be a big stunt. I wanted to ease my way back in and see if I could perform again.

The operator said it was a stunt coordinator named Joe Dunne. I'd never worked for him but knew he was from England and coordinated many of Blake Edward's films.

Teddy's connected me to Joe.

"Ello, mate," he said, "are you available tomorrow?"

I'd learned my lesson and knew enough to find out what was being asked of me.

"What are we doing, Joe?"

"Oh, it's a nothing thing for this little feature film. See you in the morning, love. I'll send the details to Teddy's."

And he hung up!

I couldn't sleep that night, worrying, wondering, watching the clock. Sean thought I was crazy for returning to the very thing that had wreaked havoc on my body. He had no inkling how much I loved being a stuntwoman. I'd tried to express my passion in countless conversations, but it was like talking to the wall. He just didn't get it.

I got to the set extra early and went sniffing around to find out what the scene was all about. I saw a huge yellow school bus and thought, *Maybe I'm driving?* My confidence in my driving was strong as ever.

Just then, I ran into my good friend Connie Palmisano and said, "Good morning, do you know what we are doing today?"

I tried to hide my nervousness with a big smile.

"Oh yeah," Connie reported, "I'm driving the bus and crashing through that wall into a movie theater. You and John Robotham will be sitting in the front row of the theater!"

He laughed.

"Hmmm," I mused, and then asked, "how likely is it that you will be able to stop the bus?"

"Be ready to run," he smirked.

I knew if anyone could stop the bus, it was Connie.

The film was *Bachelor Party* and starred Tom Hanks, a relatively unknown actor at the time.

Just then, Joe arrived. He was an elegant-looking man, well-dressed, sporting thick, silver hair. He had an air of quiet calm, and I felt comfortable around him. Well, as comfortable as my nerves would allow. Joe was happy to meet me and eager to get on with the show.

"Be ready to run," circled through my head as I inspected the bus. My running had suffered a serious setback with the shattering of my heel. But I thought that if I was about to be flattened by a bus, I just might accelerate my pace. I checked out the tires of the bus and watched the special effects guy chaining a steel cable to the axle. The cables always look way too thin to accomplish the task at hand—in this case, stopping the bus before it crushed me. The thin-as-dental-floss cable was my only hope if the bus's brakes failed, or the stuntman was asleep at the wheel.

The assistant director called the stunt folks for a meeting with the director, which meant that we were getting close. On the inside, I was a bundle of nerves; outside, I was Miss Supercool. Joe led the discussion of the action precisely in his British accent, as the director, Neil Israel, listened intently.

"Diane and John will be sitting in the front row as the bus crashes through this wall."

We were in a makeshift movie theater constructed on the lot of 20th Century Fox.

"You will remain seated until the bus comes to a stop, here."

"Here" was about three feet in front of me.

"Get ready to run" continued to race through my mind.

"Oh," Joe added, "you will be wearing 3D glasses as well."

He nearly forgot to mention that.

Oh great, I thought. *Now I can't even see straight.*

Then Neil chimed in, "Whatever you do, don't anticipate the bus not stopping, and *move*, or you will ruin the shot."

Ruin the shot or die? Is that what it boils down to?

Unfortunately, many times, it does.

On action, I was sitting in the dark theater. A movie was playing on the screen, and I had my 3D glasses on.

John, sitting next to me, said, "This is the best 3D movie I've ever seen."

I gave him a smart aleck reply of, "Eh, I've seen better."

Suddenly a punch came out of the screen, and thanks to the magic of 3D animation, it seemed to hit me in the face.

Throwing my head back, I exclaimed, "Wow!"

Just then, I heard the bus coming. It sounded like a freight train climbing the ramp to hit the wall and screen.

My legs were cocked in the "I'm out of here" position.

My head was saying, *Run you fool.*

But I didn't. As instructed, I just sat there.

Am I crazy? I wondered, feeling fairly certain I was.

No, I finally decided. *This is my job.*

CRASH!

Debris was all over me, but the bus had stopped!

Hallelujah!

I didn't move an inch.

After the smoke cleared, the director yelled, "Cut!"

Dusting myself off, I thought, *Welcome back to stunts!*

Adrenaline pumping, I was proud that I'd made it through another one unscathed.

Ironically, I won a stunt award for that scene: Best Fight Scene in a Motion Picture. They used the clip of me getting hit in the face with the punch in the movie trailer. I really got a lot of mileage out of that shot. Even today, many folks remember that striking scene.

It was great to be back! I loved the rush and had missed it tremendously.

After that job, I noticed that I started looking forward to the next "beep" that would invite me into some new adventure. My dream was once again in clear focus, and nothing could stop me now.

Word was out that I was back, and I got beeped again just a few days later. But this time I didn't panic. I was ready—mentally, and physically—for a challenge.

I was called in for an interview for *Taxi*, a big hit television show with a great cast: Judd Hirsch, Tony Danza, Danny DeVito, Andy Kaufman, Christopher Lloyd, Jeff Conaway, and Marilu Henner. *Taxi* was a sitcom and shot in front of a live studio audience. Unlike many other stunt performers, I'd earned a reputation for being able to handle dialogue. Having studied acting for years, I could handle long speeches or deliver the punch line at just the right moment. In this case, the episode was called "Jim the Psychic," and Jim (Christopher Lloyd) had a dream that Judd Hirsch was going to meet the girl of his dreams, fall in love, and two days later was going to die. There were a few other actresses and a few stuntwomen at the interview, but as I drove home that afternoon, I knew I'd nailed it. Sometimes you just get the feeling that the part is yours, and this time *it was mine*. I was thrilled to be working on this terrific hit show.

My scene was in the bar where the *Taxi* crew hung out. Jim was explaining his dream to the gang when I walked into the bar where two guys were having an argument. As I passed by them, one of the guys pushed the other guy and knocked him into me, extremely hard. I lost my balance, and the momentum catapulted me into the gang's table where I did a backflip and landed in Judd Hirsch's lap.

Shocked, I said, "I'm terribly sorry."

Tony Danza responded, "That's okay, we were expecting you."

Jim's dream was coming true.

In the dress rehearsal before the audience arrived, I split open the backside of my very tight pants as I flipped over the table. How embarrassing! I was so glad that the audience didn't see it. Of course, the cast and crew had a great belly laugh at my expense. The wardrobe lady then reinforced my pants several times.

The evening of the performance, when I arrived at my dressing room, Judd Hirsch had left me a bottle of wine with a "break a leg" message, which was so sweet of him.

As the show began, I was waiting in the wings for my cue to appear. It reminded me of the many stage plays I'd performed in during my college years. As I waited, I visualized my backflip going perfectly and me landing squarely in Judd's lap.

As I walked past the guys arguing at the bar, I noticed that they were a beat late, so I slowed my pace down and *boom*, the actor bumped into me extra hard. I adjusted my back spin to hit the table at the precise spot that I intended and flipped perfectly into the welcoming lap of Judd Hirsch.

The audience went wild, and the three cameras captured it beautifully. In fact, the producers loved the episode so much that they saved it for the opening show of the new season. I was on a roll. My career was blossoming again!

The following week I got a call from the stunt coordinator of *Crazy Like a Fox*, a television show starring Jack Warden.

Jerry Summers said, "I see you have fencing on your résumé. Can you handle an intense sword fight?"

"Absolutely," I eagerly replied.

I'd studied fencing for a few years at the University of Miami. With just a few days to prepare, I booked a lesson with the famous fencing teacher, Ralph B. Faulkner, at Faulkner's Falcon Studio in Hollywood. I'd brush up my skills and learn from the best. Mr. Faulkner taught many Hollywood greats such as Errol Flynn, Ronald Colman, Basil Rathbone, and Douglas Fairbanks, Jr.

When I arrived at the studio, I was shocked to see an incredibly old man sitting behind the enormous, cluttered, and dusty desk. Mr. Faulkner was nearly ninety years old. I told him about my experience on the University of Miami fencing team, and he explained to me that fencing in movies and television was quite different from fencing for competition.

He suddenly arose from his desk and picked up a French foil. His posture and stern visage took on another dimension as he came to life with that sword in his hand. Explaining the wide sweeping motions that needed to happen for the camera to read the action, he tossed me a sword and we began the dance. It was a magical moment. He instructed and guided me as we battled our swords around the studio. I was exhausted after a half hour of thrusting, parrying, and defending myself. He was an incredible teacher, and I learned so very much in such a short encounter with that amazing man. After the lesson, I thanked him profusely and was on my way.

A few days later, I arrived on the set with my French foil feeling super confident and ready to roll with Mr. Faulkner's wise words still echoing in my head. "Sweep wide, sweep wide!" I met the other stuntman, John Paul, who was the son of Victor Paul, another top stuntman who was known for his excellence in sword fighting. Victor had been brought in to choreograph the sword fight.

There was a long winding staircase in the corner of the set that led to a traditional-looking living room with two couches and a fireplace. The director explained that the sword fight would begin at the top of the stairs and continue into the living room. Victor instructed John and me to warm up with some exercises, and then we moved on to the staircase. I was chosen to go down the stairs backward as John was driving me heavily with his sword. Wearing fencing helmets and jackets, we rehearsed endlessly. It was difficult to step backward down a spiral staircase while defending serious blows of an oncoming sword. Because the stairs were very narrow toward the center of the spiral, I stepped back carefully and tried diligently not to tumble down the stairs.

Then, once we entered the living room, John drove me backward over the first couch, nearly knocking an expensive sculpture off a pedestal. After scaling over the second couch, I began to overtake him feverously to win the match. When we both pulled off our helmets, it was then revealed that I was a woman.

When I was raced to the emergency room after my accident, and certainly when that first grim doctor offered such a bleak prognosis, I assumed I'd never work as a stuntwoman again. My angel, Dr. Rosenfeld, had given me hope that with the right surgery and therapies I'd be able to walk normally again. Now that I was working again in stunts—not just "working," but *thriving*—was nothing short of a miracle.

No one would have blamed me if I'd decided to hang up the Red Bag of Courage for good. My injuries were more serious than most people will see in a lifetime. I'd gotten to do what I'd loved, and I might be able to find other satisfying work pursuing other jobs in the film industry. But that little voice inside, the one I'd learned to heed, had nudged me to get back to stunts. When I was summoned by Teddy's, the voice had whispered, "Go for it." And as if by divine providence, I won a stunt award to welcome me back.

Setbacks will always come in some form or fashion. But if it's *fear* that's stopping you, you need to conquer that fear and go for it.

Was I scared to work again? I sure was. But I wasn't about to let fear be the boss of me. One yes gave me confidence to say the next yes, and before I knew it, I was living the dream that gave me so much life.

12

The Dream Evolves

"Hey, Diane," I heard as I picked up the phone. "It's the Greek Tragedy!"

My old buddy and mentor from New York, Alex Stevens, announced himself using his self-assigned nickname.

"I've got some effin' great news for you," he announced. "You gotta call this guy Don Pike. He's got a big show ready to roll and he needs a chick to double Sharon Stone. I told him you were fantastic and could handle the job, for sure. Call him right away and tell him the Greek Tragedy told you to call."

Laughing hard, I thanked him and then hung up.

Alex's call was the boost I needed. Sean and I had been sitting on the couch staring at the television in icy silence. I'd noticed that we weren't making any money at the restaurant, so earlier in the week I'd decided to examine the expense bills. I was shocked to see that he'd paid ten dollars for one head of cauliflower! When I realized he was having produce delivered by a high-end produce company, I understood why the restaurant wasn't making any money. The tension was mounting between us as I began to see that he was incapable of managing money and a restaurant.

After hanging up with Alex, I dialed Don immediately, telling him that the Greek Tragedy had suggested I call.

After an agonizing silent pause, Don put the pieces together.

"Oh!" he laughed, "Alex says great things about you. Can you get over to MGM in the morning about ten, go to wardrobe, and try on the leather pants? The last stuntwoman lied about her weight and couldn't fit in the pants. Sharon had a fit when she saw the size of her stunt double. Alex said you are trim and fit. Do you still look that way?"

"Definitely," I assured him, "I work out all the time. I look great. I'll see you in the morning."

Oh God, I shouldn't have eaten that cheeseburger tonight.

Instead of being happy for me, Sean was disgusted that I wouldn't have to share his misery at the restaurant in the morning. In that season when I wasn't doing stunts, I would wait on tables or bartend to help him. After calling a waitress to replace me, I happily began to choose what I'd wear to go on my interview. I pulled out my favorite pair of skintight blue jeans and my sexy black corduroy form-fitting shirt with snaps in front. I dug out my high-heeled black leather boots and a flashy gold-buckled belt. I was ready to rock and roll. I went to sleep praying that I would fit into those leather pants!

I was so excited the next morning that I skipped breakfast, grabbing only a quick cup of coffee so that I wouldn't add one more ounce to my body weight. I hopped into my Corvette and arrived at MGM at 9:45 a.m. I told the guard that I needed to go to the set of *Allan Quatermain and the Lost City of Gold*. He directed me to Stage 10. I parked my car, brushed my hair, fixed my lipstick, and strutted through the stage door. I headed for the coffee and craft service table where you could usually find the stunt guys gathered.

Spotting a tall, silver-haired, good-looking, rugged stuntman, I inquired, “Excuse me. Are you Don Pike?”

He nodded, winked, and smiled, “You got that right.”

I stuck out my hand and said, “I’m Diane Peterson. So nice to meet you.”

He grabbed my hand and pulled me close, hugged me, and said, “This is from the Greek Tragedy.”

We had a good laugh.

Don sent me to the wardrobe department. The wardrobe lady was a nervous wreck. She told me the last stunt girl wanted her to go out and buy bigger pants.

She said, “Thank God, I think these will work for you.”

The pants were a soft buttery leather in a light olive color. I hopped into the dressing room and carefully put one leg into the pants that would be the deciding factor if I got the job. Sitting down, I slid my other leg into the supple leather. I stood up and wiggled the pants over my hips. I sucked in my tummy and tugged up the zipper. Voilà! They fit me like a glove. Spinning around, I admired my figure in the job-winning pants. I threw on the yummy suede shirt and paraded out of the dressing room.

The wardrobe lady beamed, “Oh my, those pants look like they were made for you!”

Thank God, I thought.

I marched to the set and strutted toward Don as he was eyeing me up and down.

"You got the job, Diane," he assured me, "You look great in those leather pants! You will be doubling Sharon Stone and working with Richard Chamberlain."

Wow! Richard Chamberlain was my teenage heartthrob.

"Thank you, Don. I'll see you in the morning."

I arrived bright and early on the set, which was a large cave that had a pool of bubbling gold at the base. In the ceiling of the cave, there was a track with a miner's cart attached to it. Don explained that Sharon was afraid to ride in the miner's cart, so I would be doubling her and riding in the cart with Richard. OMG! My first scene was to ride in this tiny card with Richard, my teenage crush. I could hardly believe my good luck. Richard was already in the cart as I climbed in. Feeling butterflies in my stomach, I smiled and tried to speak but the words wouldn't come out.

He grinned, stuck out his hand, and said, "Hi, I'm Richard."

I blurted out, "Hi Richard, I'm Diane. You are the first guy I ever had a crush on in my entire life. When I was thirteen, I invited you to my birthday party in New Jersey."

He laughed warmly and said, "Really? Invite me now."

He was so gracious and kind.

The golden pool bubbled ominously below. Supposedly, we were in a gold mine somewhere in South Africa. My heart was racing as I tried to concentrate on my stunt, which was about to transpire. With Richard standing only inches away from me, my mind kept thinking how handsome he was and how much I would like to kiss him. *Stop that,* I told myself.

Silencing the distraction, I began to focus only on the stunt where I had to leap from the cart moving over the treacherous sea of bubbling gold and land on a timber that was protruding out of the cave wall. The cart was going to plunge into the thick gold liquid below. Richard rode with me in the cart on all the takes preceding the leap.

Before the stunt, we met with the medical team and the hazardous material experts. They talked about safety and precautions to take in case, by accident, I missed the timber and plunged into the pit. I was advised to wear earplugs and keep my eyes closed if I fell into the gooey liquid. I would then have to swim to the exit ramp, crawl up, and be led by the hand by a safety worker who'd lead me to the makeshift shower next to the stage. There was a special solution in the shower that would get the toxic gold particles off my skin. I did not want to fall into the pool of bubbling goo! I went over the timing during the rehearsals to determine the best time to take the leap.

We shot the rehearsals with Richard next to me in the cart. For the real take, Richard's stuntman, Jon Epstein, climbed in the cart to do the stunt. He would have to leap out to safety with me as the cart plunged into the pit of bubbling gold. It was critical that we jumped from the cart at precisely the same moment. I knew and trusted John, an excellent stuntman.

When Jon asked me if I was ready, I smiled and nodded yes. The song "All I Need Is a Miracle" played in my head.

On action, I kept my eyes on the target as the cart wound its way to the path of doom. The timber was approaching rapidly, so I climbed to the top of the cart, pushed off, and leaped across the pit of bubbling gold. As I pushed off, the cart swung away from me, and I barely grabbed the timber with my two hands. I screamed, for an extra special effect, but I knew I had it. Jon jumped at exactly the same moment. When I pulled my body up on the timber, Jon was right behind me. I glanced back and he winked and smiled.

I climbed down to the soundstage and Richard ran over and gave me a kiss. Wow, what a day!

I reflected on seeing the stunt going perfectly right. Thoughts are things and they really do impact our failures and successes. In this particular stunt, I was focused on leaping from the moving cart and seeing myself grab the protruding timber. If I'd imagined tumbling into the pit of gooey gold, I'd be much more likely to do it! And even though I needed to be prepped by the medical team and hazardous material experts to know how to respond if something went wrong, my job was to visualize success. Successful completion of a stunt required that I could see it first, and then actualize it. Specifically, I needed to be *all in*.

If there's a dream in your heart that you long to achieve, I encourage you to visualize success. Take time to focus on what the best possible outcome for your dream would look like. It might be improved physical, relational, emotional, spiritual, or financial health. Or you might be in the process of building something that doesn't yet exist. Or you're launching an idea or a new product. You will be best equipped to succeed when you can visualize success and then give your all to achieving it.

A wonderful perk of the world of stunts was that one job could lead to another. While I was working on *Quartermain*, I had a sword fight to do with stuntman Bob Minor. Bob was the stunt coordinator for *Magnum, P.I.* Bob was a well-accomplished stunt coordinator and a lot of fun to work with. On breaks between rehearsing the sword fight as we sat and chatted, I told him that I loved Ferraris and that I was saving to buy one for myself someday.

A few months after filming ended, Teddy's called and said Bob Minor was on the line. When they connected me, Bob said, "Diane, how would you like to fly to Hawaii and drive the *Magnum* Ferrari in a chase scene?"

"Are you kidding?" I exploded, "I'd love to!" I had innocently planted the seed for this job when I told him about my love of Ferraris.

Bob explained that in the episode, a girl steals the Magnum Ferrari, and the chase ensues. I was so thrilled; I could hardly wait. I flew to Oahu, Hawaii and early the following morning went directly to the set.

Handing me the keys, Bob said, "Take it for a spin and get used to the handling."

I had driven my brother's Ferrari on the track at Lime Rock, Connecticut, so I had experience driving a Ferrari fast. The *Magnum* Ferrari was a 308 GTS. I felt ready as ever to begin the chase. While I was waiting, Tom Selleck came over to say hello. I just sat there thinking, how lucky am I? Driving a Ferrari in a chase scene in Hawaii and meeting Tom Selleck. I love this job!

I was sent to the hair and makeup department, and a very unattractive wig was plopped on my head. I was ready for action.

As the chase began, I had several cop cars hot on my tail, as well as a helicopter following in the air with a cameraman hanging outside and filming the action. I had a radio tucked between my legs to listen to the director as I shifted the purring Ferrari and slid around corners. It was so responsive. We moved as one. There were several nondescript cars added on the streets that I could weave in and out of as I maneuvered the sharp turns. The Ferrari hugged the road as the sirens of the cop cars filled my ears. I can still remember the thrill like it was yesterday.

Because filming a scene such as this takes quite a long time, I was in Hawaii for a week, and it was one of the most enjoyable jobs I was ever blessed to have. I will always be grateful that Bob listened to my story of loving Ferraris and then remembered me when this episode turned up.

I filmed that episode in 1987. In 1997, ten years later, I ordered my 1998 Ferrari 355 GTS! Dreams do come true if you believe in them.

13

Life's Mysteries

After Dar Robinson had hit the guardrail on his motorcycle faster than I thought he was planning on, I watched as he flew through the air like a ragdoll and—unbelievably—landed on a pile of cardboard boxes exactly where he'd placed an X mark.

It was a few days before Thanksgiving in 1986. Our Los Angeles gang of approximately twenty stuntpeople had been hired to perform motorcycle stunts and car chases in Page, Arizona for *Million Dollar Mystery*. Vic Armstrong was the second unit director for all the action sequences, and my good friend George Fisher was the stunt coordinator. We were staying at the Wahweap Lodge, strategically placed on the shores of gorgeous Lake Powell. The vast blue lake was surrounded by sandstone walls that changed colors as the sun slowly glided across the cloudless sky. It was an idyllic location, peaceful with natural beauty in every direction.

On the first day of shooting, the scorching sun was beating down on my frumpy brown wig. The style looked early fifties with a not-so-cute little flip. I was dressed in a red checkered blouse, tan A-line skirt, and brown suede cowboy boots. Someone said I looked like Patsy Kline, but I felt like Dale Evans. It's funny, I actually wanted to be Roy Rogers's wife, Dale, when I was a little kid! I looked the part for sure. My job was to ride passenger with a stunt guy who was always screwing up. It's not easy to just belt up, be quiet and hang on—and in this case, watch the disaster unfold. Fortunately for me, the disasters were minor, such as sliding into a car that we were to nearly miss, hitting a curb, and blowing out a tire. I so wished that I was the driver, but I was grateful for the work.

In the story, we are all in a diner when a patron announces, on his dying breath, that he hid a million dollars. He gave us a set of clues, and we all ran off like maniacs to find the cash and keep it. We raced past the Rainbow Bridge, the world's largest natural stone bridge, and headed into the Arizona desert.

The next morning, Dar Robinson, a stuntman famous for his high falls, was preparing for his exciting motorcycle stunt. He was to drive his motorcycle at approximated thirty-five miles per hour into a guardrail on a curved mountaintop road. He would then catapult himself off the bike, fly through the air about seventy-five feet, and land flat on his back in a sea of cardboard boxes. The night before, I asked him how he figured out where he was going to land. He proceeded to give me a lengthy explanation using a slide rule to show me how he calculated precisely where he was going to land. Most stunt guys would not divulge how they planned their stunts for fear that you might steal their idea. Dar happily shared his knowledge, which I thought was so cool.

The emergency helicopter was standing by just in case his calculation was incorrect. We all stood by, waiting and praying. My faith always settled me down in times like this with tension mounting. I heard the roar of the motorcycle. After hitting the guardrail, Dar landed directly on the box where he marked the X. I was elated! I jumped up and down and cheered along with the crowd.

Rolling off the boxes, Dar shook his head and said, "I want to do one more. I can go higher."

I thought to myself, *That was perfect. Why do another one?* But Dar said he was going to put pegs at the base of the motorcycle seat and push off as he was ejected from the motorcycle. On take two, Dar sailed even higher though the air and landed exactly on target once again. Amazing! We all congratulated Dar and began our journey back to the hotel. The emergency helicopter also took off. Dar and two other stuntmen stayed behind to complete some run-bys, a shot when the camera is stationary and the motorcycles fly past the camera.

I arrived back at the hotel and went to the lounge with my good friend, Dana. We usually had a drink or two when we finished working. We were laughing about my stupid-looking wig when a production assistant with a sullen, expressionless face appeared at the door.

A chill went through my body as I asked, "What's up with you, Joe?"

Joe sadly explained, "There was an accident. Dar slid off the cliff on his motorcycle."

I said, "That's not possible. We were on set. The stunt went great!"

"No, after you guys left. The three stuntmen were doing runs by the camera, and Dar was on the outside. He hit some gravel and slid off the cliff. He fell about forty feet to the desert floor. He got gored in his side by the desert brush. The helicopter and ambulance were gone. We had to carry him to the back of the SUV and race to the hospital. He bled to death on the way there."

Oh my God. Another friend to lose his life for a stupid movie. Was it worth it?

Remembering the fateful day when Vic died on the set of *Hi-Riders,* I felt shattered inside.

The producers called the cast and crew into the convention center the next morning. Dana and I were in shock and couldn't sleep all night. After silently walking past Dar's Corvette parked outside, we were like walking zombies entering the cold, cavernous room. Everyone there was so deeply saddened. Dana and I held hands and cried. The producers tried to explain the "freak accident" that occurred the afternoon before.

Freak accident? Aren't all accidents freakish?

The producers explained that when Dar fell from the side of the cliff, the desert brush found the one spot where he was unprotected and punctured his side. He was wearing a helmet and a chest protector. Without the helicopter and ambulance standing by, there was no choice but to make a desperate run by car to the nearest hospital some seventy-five miles away.

The angry crowd shouted, "Why were the helicopter and ambulance let go?"

The producer explained that the big stunts were over for that day and that is why they were released. However, on a remote location like that, the helicopter and ambulance should have remained until the shooting was completed. I suspect budget concerns had a lot to do with the decision that was made to let them go.

Dar died before they reached the hospital. He was only thirty-nine years old. He had a cute, blond little boy who looked just like him. A little boy who would never get to know his dad. As I thought about Dar's family, I began to examine my life and decided that it was indeed time for me to get serious about having a baby. After all, I was thirty-five years old, and the biological clock was ticking fast. I'd talked about having a baby with Sean and he always put it off saying, "When we get our house, then we'll have a kid." We had our house now. Now with the death of my four friends—Vic Rivers, A.J. Bakunas, Jack Tyree, Dar Robinson—and my serious injury, I felt life longing for itself deep inside me.

When Sean came to visit me at the Wahweap Lodge, I told him that I really wanted to take a break from work and try to have our baby. But after I shared my heart, Sean said the restaurant had closed! That was no big surprise; he really didn't know how to manage it. And, once again, he didn't have a job.

The rest of the shoot went fine on the movie, but there was a somber air of sadness that permeated the atmosphere.

As soon as I returned home, Teddy's called me. My services were becoming much in demand. After all, I was the president of the Stuntwomen's Association of Motion Pictures, a position I held for seven years. Being the president was a joy because I believed in our group. It was wonderful to network with like-minded women and share our knowledge and experience. Wanting to serve our members, I organized some learning seminars for us such as repelling and white-water rafting.

The call from Teddy's was from a stunt coordinator named Chuck Courtney. I had heard his name before, but I'd never worked for him. He told me that my friend Donna Garrett put my name in for the job. Donna and I were about the same size, and she was kind enough to recommend me for jobs that she did not want or was unavailable to do. This job was for several weeks in Vancouver, Canada. Donna had two kids and was a single parent, so she did not want to leave them alone for that long. This was a television series based on the movie *Stir Crazy*, which starred Gene Wilder and Richard Pryor. A series is fabulous work, especially if you are doubling the lead, which is what I was called in to do. The character was named Captain Betty, and she wore chrome cowboy boots and drove a chrome cop car. Chuck said there would be a lot of action for me, so I agreed immediately. Sean, who managed to get fired from every job he had, and lost the restaurant, was still out of work. I really wanted a baby, but we needed the money for the new house we had just purchased. It seemed that I wanted a baby much more than he. Knowing I could bring in some big bucks with this show, I prepared my Red Bag of Courage for my journey. I must admit that I really looked forward to the adventure. I had never been to Vancouver, and I had heard wonderful things about the city. Sean didn't seem fazed much in any way when I told him the news. Cracks had been beginning to form in our marriage. Maybe I just needed to get away and think things through.

I arrived in Canada and met Chuck, a short, red-faced, chubby, nervous cowboy. He said we needed to go to the park and check out our first stunt, together, in which he would "thread the needle" with a cop car. "Threading the needle" meant that he had to land the airborne cop car between two trees. I would be sitting in the passenger seat. Ugh! I hated riding passenger. Arriving at an incredibly beautiful, lush, green park, we marched over to two towering trees that were about six feet apart. Chuck explained that he was going to hit a ramp to send us airborne and then fly through the air and land wedged between the two trees. He nervously said there would be a cable to stop us at the precise spot that he mapped out.

I couldn't stand near Chuck too long because he was so nervous it made me uncomfortable. Turning to silent prayer, I began padding up. I strapped on shin guards, kneepads, elbow pads, wet suit vest with chest protector, and my mouthpiece. I did not want to crack those pearly whites! I walked around and envisioned the stunt going right, but it was out of my control. I was a sitting duck in the passenger seat.

"Let's go, Peterson!" Chuck yelled.

I belted myself in the five-piece harness, tried to relax, and waited for action. On action, Chuck floored the gas on the cop car, hit the ramp, and in midair the car turned and all I saw was the tree coming directly at me. I braced for impact, and *whack!* We hit the tree nearly head-on, on my side. I was stunned. My neck began to ache immediately.

Chuck was silent, speechless. I could feel the depth of his embarrassment.

Medics ran in. "Are you okay? Are you okay?"

"Uh . . . I think so," I stammered, trying to slowly move my neck around.

Rescuers pried my door open with the Jaws of Life, and I crawled out of the severely crushed vehicle.

"What happened?" I asked the medic.

He walked me to the back of the car and showed me that the cable got caught on the end of the ramp and threw the car sideways.

Good thing I'm not pregnant.

I could see how upset and embarrassed Chuck was, so I decided to leave him alone. I know all too well that when a stunt goes awry the last thing you want to do is talk to anyone and try to explain. You really just want to crawl in a hole and disappear.

My neck was really sore for a few days, but I was grateful that my injures were not worse than that.

Vancouver was much more beautiful than I ever imagined. The rich hunter green of the well-manicured lawns was decorated with a kaleidoscope of vibrant flowers. My character, Captain Betty, maneuvered a lot of car chases in her chrome cop car and performed many other crazy stunts that the writers dreamed up. I just loved my chrome cowboy boots and laughed at my memories of being Sheriff Randal as a kid and running around in my red cowboy boots. Now I was being paid quite well to have the same kind of fun, in an adult way. As the days wore on, I got do more and more exciting stunts, which kept my mind from worrying about Sean getting a job and my longing for a baby. I executed flawless 180-degree turns in car chases and did side slides that looked like an ice ballet. There is nothing I loved more than a great car chase.

On one episode, I drove a Ford Falcon in a chase and hit a ramp and sailed through the air for about twenty feet before plunging into a lake. Since it was television, they wanted the car to sink fast, so they took out the floorboards and installed mesh wiring. When I hit the water, in two seconds, I was up to my neck in water as the car rapidly sunk. I struggled to release my seat belt, and I escaped at the last possible moment. Naturally I couldn't help but think of Vic and his last precious moments of life. Rising to the water's surface, I gave a thumbs-up to the safety divers who were poised and ready to jump in if I was in trouble. Thank God, this time they were not needed.

The writers also dreamed up a wild stunt with a toboggan on wheels. As Captain Betty was chasing the bad guys once again, she spotted a unique toboggan on the top of a mercilessly steep mountain. Betty hopped in the toboggan for the ride of her life, trying to catch the bad guys on the run. On the way down the mountain, I would hit a ramp and sail through the air. The editor would cut the film and have me landing on top of a ski tram thousands of feet above the ground. However, for the actual stunt, I really had to land the toboggan by hitting the ground. No one knew exactly how far I would go or what would happen. This stunt had never been done before. So, I padded up like the Michelin Man once again with every pad I owned. All the stuntmen were at the bottom of the hill and promised to stop me if I continued on a path to smash into the trees that lurked behind them. I was boiling hot in my police outfit with the myriad of pads strapped to my body. I asked the medic how far the nearest hospital was, and he said ten minutes away.

Pausing to relax and visualize the stunt going perfectly, I said, "I'm ready, let's shoot this."

On action, Chuck pushed my toboggan as hard and fast as he could. I was off and racing down the hill, full speed ahead. I hit the ramp square in the middle as planned and was catapulted into midair. I saw the stunt guys running away from the trees, scattering like mice. They were doing an "olé" like the bullfighters, leaving me on my own for when I hit the ground and raced toward them. I came down hard and saw the trees rapidly approaching. Somehow, I managed to fling myself off the toboggan sideways, and the toboggan crashed head-on into a mighty oak. The stunt guys ran over to help me up and were laughing.

"There was no way that we could stop you," they roared, "so we bailed!"

Thanks a lot, I thought to myself.

I was just happy that I was in one piece and that there was no second take.

We then moved to the Grouse Mountain Tram which glided four thousand feet up the side of a mountain. I had to sit on top of the tram strapped to my toboggan and attached by a thread of a cable. Honestly, the cable looked as thin as a guitar string, and I wondered if it was enough to hold me securely.

The cable operator tried to scare me and said, "Be ready to hold on tight, if I have to slam the brakes on, there's a twenty-foot whip in the cable."

I remained calm and asked, "How likely is it that you will have to do that?"

"Not too likely," he chuckled.

As the tram rose up the mountain, I sang "Ain't No Mountain High Enough" and didn't look down. Remember, heights were not my friend. I just kept singing and looking at the blue sky with the dreamy clouds floating by. We had to do the run three times and thank God the cable operator never had to slam the brakes on!

I did several other odd and unusual stunts in the coming weeks, including hitting a logjam with a speedboat and sailing over the top of it. Now that was one crazy ride. I hung onto the steering wheel and rode that boat like it was a wild pony. The boat nearly flipped over!

In another scene, we were in a fish hatchery doing a foot chase, and they released a ton of slippery fish onto the floor. Trying to run through them was a joke. Falling down and getting up was like sliding on a greased frying pan with hundreds of halibut surrounding your feet. And the smell was unbearable. All in a day's work. Conquering the unexpected and living to laugh about it later was part of the joy of my job.

When we were finished filming, we were sent on our way home, not knowing if the series would be picked up for more shows. I had mixed feelings about continuing with the show if it got picked up because I had other things on my mind.

When I'd returned to Hollywood after Vic's death, I'd fully committed myself to living out my dream of doing stunts. And yet another possibility kept nagging at me. *Was a baby calling?* It was a possibility that I couldn't *not* consider. Just as my dream had taken one detour, I wondered if it might be time for another detour. I knew I needed to fully explore the gravity of my pull in another direction. The clock was ticking.

Sometimes the dream we were meant to live includes diversions. Maybe you'll pause to pursue the education or training you need in order to do what you were made to do. Or you might slow down for the sake of a relationship: caring for a loved one who is ill, adding a child to your life, or pursuing a new relationship. And it could be that an interruption you never would have chosen has disrupted the trajectory you anticipated. Pursuing your dream doesn't preclude diversions, but those diversions need not derail your dream.

I didn't know yet whether the possibility I held in my heart would interrupt my dream, but I wanted to explore it.

During this season, there was a big splash about me in a number of magazines. Dewar's scotch whiskey had an amazing campaign of interesting people for their full-page ads, and I was chosen to be Dewar's 100th Profile as the stuntwoman they wanted to profile. It was quite an honor. First, they flew me to Chicago and shot me physically busting through a breakaway wall. Then sitting in a director's chair with a glass of Dewar's. Then they changed art directors and reshot the ad with me looking extremely glamorous in a black sexy gown perched on a small ledge outside a Gothic-looking window. I loved the photo, but the copy that they wrote was absolutely nothing that I said in the interviews. They reported that I'd called my "most fearless act" to be "discussing politics at a dinner party in California." Now there's something I'd never do!

14

The Opportunity I Didn't See Coming

I arrived home in Simi Valley from my Canadian adventure in the spring of 1986. I was excited about starting a family. I even had an artist paint a large, cute bunny mural on the wall in the room reserved for a baby.

Sean finally got hired as a property manager at a large apartment complex. Another nine-to-five job that didn't pay much, but at least he was working. When I was between jobs, my life consisted of getting up and going to the gym, riding my motorcycle, or riding my neighbor's Peruvian Paseo stallion, Stormy. I also went to the movies to study my craft and see the newest stunts that were getting better and more outrageous than ever before.

Sean's attitude and behavior signaled that he was jealous of the freedom I enjoyed.

Each morning he would mutter, "What are you doing today, Diane?" as he primped his hair into a perfect bouffant.

"I'm hitting the gym, hustling for work, and riding Stormy," I would say as I grabbed my gym bag and headed for the door.

"At least *one* of us is working," he would jab.

I tried not to let the verbal dagger upset the joy in my heart for the day ahead. I loved my job whenever I worked and counted it as a real blessing that I found something that I loved to do and got paid incredibly well whenever I did work. And the residuals coming in continued to be an extra bonus. Between jobs, I worked at staying in shape, hunting for the next job, and enjoying life. Knowing the next job was just a phone call away, I kept following my dream.

Between assignments, I designed a boulder swimming pool with a waterfall into the hot tub for our castle on the hill. I would swim, and float, and dream of the family that would fill my new home in the hills of Simi Valley, imagining a little boy and a little girl running and laughing in the yard with a dog chasing at their heels. I was willing to take some time off to have children, as some of my friends had done. I longed for the perfect loving family.

One evening, Sean told me his office was having a Christmas party and said that I didn't have to come if I didn't want to. I said that I would love to go, but I felt reluctance on his part to have me accompany him. Still, I got ready and hopped in the car with him.

"Who's that blond staring at you?" I asked Sean as we danced at the party in the Greek restaurant.

"Oh, that's Kelly, my new secretary, you'll have to meet her," he sheepishly replied.

I can hardly wait.

We walked over to her, and Sean introduced us.

Kelly gushed with fake niceness, "I've heard so much about you. It's soo nice to meet you."

Grabbing Sean's hand, I dragged him onto the dance floor. He was a great dancer. Ha! It was one of the shallow reasons I married him. Feeling uncomfortable with Kelly's beady eyes on my back, I told him I was tired and wanted to leave. I felt that the woman was evil, but I couldn't share that with my husband. After all, she was his secretary, and he seemed very pleased about that.

The next day I was cruising down the Pacific Coast Highway in my red Corvette daydreaming and singing along with the radio. I was abruptly brought back to earth by the welcome sound of my pager. It was music to my ears. Feeling like I was Clark Kent about to change into a superhero in the telephone booth, I immediately searched for a gas station and a phone.

Teddy's told me a producer from Warner Brothers was trying to reach me about a movie called *Her Secret Life*.

They connected me and he said, "We are doing a movie in Mexico starring Kate Capshaw. I was told that you would make a good double for her and that you could possibly stunt coordinate as well."

My mind raced.

Mexico. I do make a great double for Kate. I can coordinate.

"Send me the script," I suggested, "and I'll break it down."

The script arrived the next day by messenger. I dove into the script, carefully reading each scene and marking down the stunts. I planned how many people I would need and how much the stunt adjustments would cost. There was a huge gun battle scene that would require about fifty guys. I would also be doubling Kate escaping from a mansion by swinging on a vine and doing water work at night. I would be escaping from Cuba (supposedly) and searchlights would skim the water looking for me. I needed to pad the budget a little because circumstances when filming could require extra action sequences. I really wanted the job. I loved to stunt coordinate, and those jobs were few and far between for women at the time.

I arrived well prepared to meet the producers. When I walked in the room, they all looked at one another and nodded their heads.

"You make a great double for Kate. Let's see what you have there for a budget."

The producer glanced at the budget and said, "You have the job, but you have to hire all the stunt guys as locals in Mexico."

Believing I could bring several stuntmen from Los Angeles, I quickly said, "I don't speak Spanish."

"Don't worry, we'll have an interpreter for you. We are shooting in Veracruz. We need you there on Monday to hire about forty guys and teach them how to fall on cue when they get shot."

"You got it!" I fired back.

Monday, I flew to Mexico City and then boarded a tiny plane to Veracruz. A guy with an enormous mustache was at the airport holding a sign with my name on it.

He didn't speak much English, so I just enjoyed the scenery as we drove to the hotel. I checked in and was immediately ushered into a ballroom where seventy-five Mexican guys were all waiting to meet me. It was a bit overwhelming and sad to have all those needy eyes looking at me, pleading for a job.

I met José, my trusty interpreter, and told him to send five guys in at a time.

I explained, "Please write their names down. I will show them what I want. They need to take a bullet hit and fall down on one of the floor mats. I will mark a check next to the guys that will remain."

I needed about forty guys, ten featured and the rest background. I introduced myself to the first five, my words being echoed in Spanish by José. I demonstrated to the group getting hit by a bullet and falling to the ground.

There was much snickering and snorting going on until I pointed at the first guy and said, "Bang!"

He looked stunned, grabbed his chest, and sat down.

No bueno.

The next guy, a big fat Mexican who'd clearly had too many cervezas over the years, stepped onto the mat.

"Bang!" I yelled. He grabbed his chest, flipped over, and landed on his head.

"Bueno," I said and gave him a thumbs-up.

And so it went till I had my full cast of characters.

The next day, we arrived at the airport location. The guys were dressed and ready for action when I arrived. I placed them strategically around the buildings for the shoot-out. José explained my every word to them. After several rehearsals, we were ready to shoot. On action, the gunfire began, and the guys were hitting the ground as rehearsed, beautifully.

But before the director yelled cut, two guys who were supposed to be dead moved! I guess that instruction was lost in translation. Thankfully, we managed to get the scene done perfectly by the end of the day. The guys worked hard and deserved what little pay they did receive.

On another scene, the special effects coordinator worked with me on making the vine that I would need to swing on to escape from the mansion. He did a terrific job of making the vine look realistic so that I could run along the rooftop of a building, grab the vine, swing to the ground, and escape from the bad guys who were chasing me.

The next night I had to go into the water by the docks. Noticing the water appeared to be polluted, I talked to the medic. He rummaged around his medical bag and pulled out some protective eyedrops that looked ancient. I examined the bottle and they'd expired five years ago. No way I was putting those drops in my eyes. After sending an assistant to the pharmacy to get fresh drops, I put ear plugs in my ears and was ready to face the black lagoon.

In the scene, Kate was escaping from Cuba, so I needed the beams of the searchlights skimming the water to miss me as I dove under the water each time they approached. The water was warm like a bathtub! The job turned out fantastic and I loved Veracruz.

When I'd caught the "stunt bug" in New York, I wanted nothing more than to drive and do car chases. At that time, I couldn't have anticipated the other opportunities that would come my way as a result of pursuing my passion. And yet along the way I'd been offered opportunities to both perform and coordinate stunts. With every new opportunity, I'd had to make the decision to accept the challenge. And by saying yes, I was learning, growing, and expanding both my skill set and my résumé.

As you're pursuing your dream, you may be offered opportunities you couldn't have seen coming. If you're working as an extra on the set, you might meet a stunt coordinator who will give you a break. If you're working as an editor, you may be given the chance to write. If you're working as an assistant director, you might notice an opportunity to direct. When these opportunities come your way, you can choose to grow and develop by rising to the occasion.

Be ready to say *yes*!

My next yes, a fairly easy one, was about to take an unusual turn.

Entering a darkened barroom at seven o'clock in the morning, the stench of stale cigarettes and spilled whiskey made me feel nauseated.

I'd been called to double Faye Dunaway on the film *Barfly* starring Mickey Rourke. I arrived on the set, which was a very seedy bar in Culver City. There was a plethora of hungover-looking extras hovering over the sticky bar. The lights were dim, and I searched to find the stunt coordinator, Webster Whinery, and the director, Barbet Schroeder. I spotted them discussing the scene in the corner of the disheveled barroom.

The director explained to me that Faye walks into the bar and sees Mickey talking to another woman on the barstool next to him. In a jealous rage, Faye begins a fight with the woman by pulling her off the barstool backward by her hair.

Cool. Sounds like a rip-roaring brawl.

He explained that he wanted me to cover the full room: fighting over tables, chairs, booths, and rolling around on the floor in a massive catfight.

When they sent me to hair and makeup, we discovered my hair was pretty close to Faye's hair in color and length, so they just needed to mess it up. I needed to look like I was that deranged woman on the three-day bender. Pretty scary makeup, too. Smeared lipstick and smudged eyeliner! Beside me, the stuntwoman who I would be fighting with, Debby Lyn Ross, was getting a long brown wig pinned on her scalp. Having worked with Debby before, who was terrific, I knew we could give them what they were looking for.

After being fitted in some funky, old, shabby clothes, I entered the dismal bar, ready to rumble. We did a slow speed rehearsal several times and plotted the moves around the room to cover all corners. When Webster asked us if we were ready to go, we both nodded yes.

On action, I walked into the bar and spotted Mickey talking to the other woman. They were sitting next to each other way too close on barstools. Walking slowly over to her, I wrapped my hand around her long brown ponytail and yanked her backward off the bar stool. To my amazement, her wig came off in my hand! I did not hear "cut," so I continued to fight. The stuntwoman had no wig on, just a head full of bobby pins. I smashed tables and chairs and rolled around on the floor with her until finally Barbet yelled as loud as he could, "Cut!"

Everyone laughed so hard. It was truly hilarious. Needless to say, her wig got plastered to her head for the next take. The fight turned out amazing, and the wig in my hand was a funny moment! One that I'll never forget.

A few days later, I got a call from stunt coordinator Jophrey Brown to work on the feature film *Action Jackson* starring Carl Weathers and Craig T. Nelson. I was asked to double Sharon Stone as I had done before. Jophrey asked me if I had been thrown through a window before. I told him I had done windows many times and I that I was available.

I arrived on the set, and there was an enormous floor-to-ceiling window staring at me. The glass was tempered. When tempered glass shatters, it shatters into thousands of tiny, sharp pieces. Candy glass is only used on smaller windows as it breaks easily. If the window is large, the candy glass must be very thick, and it looks fake. I actually prefer the tempered glass because the candy glass can break into large shards that stab you in delicate places.

On action, another stuntman hurled me toward the ominous window. I went with the force of the push and tried to protect my eyes and face with my arm as I sailed toward the giant window. Special effects men remotely hit a button that pronged the glass to stir up the molecules before I hit the window to enable it to break. I hit the window hard, crashed through it, and flipped onto my back as I slid through the millions of shards of glass.

I laid still and waited to hear "cut" from the director. I knew to keep my eyes closed as I could feel the glass all over my face.

I finally heard "cut" and put my thumb up as the medic ran in with a small air gun to blast the debris off my face.

"Are you okay? Keep your eyes closed," the medic calmly said.

I nodded yes, and he blew the remaining debris off my face. My hands were aching and as I raised them up, blood gushed all over me.

He took one look at my hands and said, "We are going to the hospital. I can't get all this glass out of your hands here."

I didn't want to go to the hospital, but I reluctantly agreed. I knew those trips to the hospital were lengthy and I just wanted to get home, though I knew my hands needed work and I was in pain for sure.

Jophrey came over to assure me that I'd done a fabulous job. And he acknowledged that the trip to the hospital was a necessity.

The emergency room doc was young and handsome. He reminded me of the Dr. Kildare character played by Richard Chamberlain. He asked me what happened, and I told him that I flung myself through a window. He looked at me like I was a psycho and then I laughed and told him that I was a stuntwoman.

"Wow! I never met a stuntwoman before," he gushed, "Would you like to have dinner sometime?"

"I'd love to, but I'm married, so I'll have to pass," I smiled.

He carefully extracted the shards of glass out of my two hands after giving me some pain medication. I was not able to drive home so I called Sean and told him that I was in the hospital.

"What the hell happened to you now?" he barked.

I told him I got glass in my hands, and I couldn't drive home because I was on medication and my hands were bandaged. But because I'd interrupted the movie he was watching on television, he was annoyed.

"This movie has another half hour to go. I'll come for you when it's over."

And he slammed the phone down.

Boy, that doc was looking better by the moment.

15

An Exciting Opportunity

I was recuperating from my injuries, relaxing at my gorgeous boulder pool, when the phone rang and woke me from my daydream of having a little one running around my backyard.

It was Don Pike who said, "Hey blondie, how's it going?"

"Oh, I cut my hands going through a window on *Action Jackson,*" I explained, "but I'll be okay," I laughed.

"Don't you know you never drag your hands after crashing through a window?" he chuckled.

Obviously, he had done the same thing before. There is nothing like experience to teach you hard lessons.

"I know now," I confirmed. "What's up?"

Don always had interesting projects coming his way and I loved working with him.

"How would you like to go to South Africa for a couple months? I'm doing an Indiana Jones type movie called *River of Death*, and they don't have any stuntwomen over there."

I wasn't sure if he was joking or not. Don was a prankster.

"There's going to be a lot of good stunts for you, and you can make a ton of money," he continued, "What do ya say?"

"Wow," I marveled, "Don, that sounds super cool, but I need to run it by Sean."

"Okay, I'll send you the script," he answered. "Let me know ASAP."

That evening, I decided to cook up a batch of Sean's favorite soup that I made from my mom's old Polish recipe. The house smelled amazing from the aroma of the Polish red tomato, vegetable, and beef soup. A fire was roaring in the fireplace, and I put on a sexy little outfit of Daisy Mae shorts and a midriff top.

Sean walked in and said, "Umm, smells good in here."

When I kissed him, he was cold as a glacier. I returned to stirring my soup and told him that I'd gotten a call from Don Pike.

"Yeah," he inquired, "what's up with him?"

"He's got a film deal called *The River of Death* shooting in South Africa, and he wants me to go for a couple of months. What do you think?"

"How much money will you make?" he quickly replied.

I stopped stirring the soup and asked, "Is that all you care about?"

As exciting as the project sounded, I so wished that Sean would have said, "Please don't go, honey. Stay home and we'll make that baby that we have been trying for."

We'd been trying to conceive without success. Sean had a low sperm count and, to improve our chances, the doctor had told him to stay out of the hot tub, wear boxer shorts, and quit drinking. None of which he chose to do. Although in vitro fertilization was just being introduced, I felt that if we were meant to have a baby, we'd conceive one naturally. I didn't want to play God. Despite my longing that Sean would ask me to stay, he was happy to let me go.

When the script arrived the very next day by courier, I tore right into it. It was filled with high-action scenes of explosions, chases, and helicopter work.

Then I read:

"The girl is running through the jungle when a giant fourteen-foot boa constrictor falls on her and begins to wrap its body around her screaming, trembling frame."

Oh my God, I can't do this. There is no way I can do this.

I hate snakes, and the thought of one enormous boa wrapped around my body was overwhelmingly repulsive and frigging scary. When it comes to overcoming my fears in regard to heights and fire, I can psych myself up for the challenge. But snakes are an entirely different matter. The snake was all I could think about while I read the remainder of the script. I tried to focus on the cool things that I would be doing—driving jeeps, racing through the jungle, playing a pirate woman, and doubling the lead actress whenever she could not or would not do some bit of action. Including the snake fiasco! It all sounded fun and doable, but the thought of the snake strangling me and crushing me to death as the snake handler stood by—not wanting to kill his pet snake—filled my mind. The hero, Michael Dudikoff, was supposed to save me by pulling the snake off me in the final seconds of my life.

Elated for the opportunity, I tried to focus on all of the positive benefits of accepting the job. The adventure of a journey to a foreign, unknown country lit my fire. I looked at a map of the world and located the tiny little town called Port St. Johns on the coast of South Africa that would be my home for several months. When else would I ever get a chance to experience life on that magical part of the planet? The money was great. I was offered $3,000 a week, plus stunt adjustments. Sean was encouraging to me to go. He was happy I would make plenty of money, and he assured me that we could work on having a baby when I returned. Though I was still disappointed he didn't ask me to stay home to work on baby-making, at least I had his agreement that we would get to it upon my return.

The big question remained: Could I endure the snake thing?

I suppose I have this "go for it" switch inside my brain and once triggered there is no stopping me. I thought about my fear of heights and how I'd been able to overcome that long enough to get the shot, but could I allow the massive slimy snake to wrap around my body and squeeze me?

The gauntlet was thrown; the challenge was at my feet. Because I knew the best way to overcome fear was to face it head-on, I made the call to Don Pike.

"I'm in, Don. See you in South Africa."

The moment I hung up the phone, I had a flash of Mr. Boa strangling me to death as everyone stood around dumbfounded, not knowing what to do! I tried to dismiss those thoughts and replace them with images of tranquil white-sand beaches on the South African shore. Before long, though, I began having nightmares of Mr. Boa and waking up screaming and sweating.

My husband would just simply say, "Be quiet, don't worry about it, go back to sleep." Never once did he say the words I longed to hear, "Forget the job. Just stay home, baby."

Perhaps he was calculating the insurance money that he would get upon my demise.

The waiting seemed endless. But finally, the day arrived to begin my journey to the other side of the world. My route was to fly from Los Angeles to London, then on to a stop in Nairobi, Kenya, and next to Johannesburg, South Africa—Jo'burg as it is known to the locals. The final flight was to the small city of Umtata in the Eastern Cape province of South Africa.

When Sean drove me to LAX, there were no teary goodbyes at the airport. In fact, I sensed that he was happy I was going, but I didn't know from where that feeling was coming.

Nervous and excited to finally be on my way, it was always fun to be flying first class. However, I couldn't eat or sleep much because I had the snake drama replaying itself in my head. It took a full day and a half to reach Jo'burg where I was met with a tiny propeller plane. There were cages of chickens being loaded into the miniature plane and a pilot who looked too young to even drive a car! As the only white face waiting to board, the other few passengers stared at me, seeming to question what I was doing in their neck of the woods. The flight was bumpy and choppy, and I began to wonder if I would ever see Port St. Johns after all. We came down hard on the tarmac and bounced into Umtata with chickens squawking and passengers screaming. Spotting a small shack that was the airport headquarters, I exited the plane and noticed a very old Black man with a tattered, floppy hat and a huge toothless grin holding a sign with my name on it. *Thank God someone is here to meet me in the middle of nowhere.* I'd been told that I was only allowed two small bags because of this tiny plane, so I picked up my two duffle bags and crawled into the back of the *kombi* (what the locals called a van). I was exhausted from the journey, and we still had another three hours to travel over the pothole-filled roads. The old beat-up kombi bounced and rattled to the sound of South African music blaring loudly in my ears from the radio. I tried to rest but I couldn't keep my eyes off the hordes of Black women walking along the roadside, carrying huge loads of rice and flour sacks on their heads. There were pigs, donkeys, dogs, and turbaned native folks all roaming the dusty roadway.

As we passed countless round stone houses with thatched roofs, I asked the driver why the houses were all round.

He just smiled at me with his toothless grin and said, "Evil spirits dwell in corners. Didn't you know that?"

Despite the plethora of Polish superstitions I'd learned, my mother never taught me that one!

Finally, we arrived at a quaint white two-story hotel by the sea. A Black woman was scrubbing the floors on her hands and knees as we entered the tiny lobby. After checking in, I dropped my bags in my sparse, miniature room. I'd asked my driver to wait for me because I wanted to go to the set and talk to the director, Steve Carver. I was dead tired, but I had to find out when in the hell we were going to shoot the snake scene. I prayed that it would be *soon* so that I could then relax and get some much-needed sleep. I was so tired of the snaky, frightening nightmares.

Arriving at the set somewhere in the middle of the jungle, I spotted Steve and strolled over to see him. I had worked with him before, so he greeted me with a huge hug.

"I'm so glad you're here Diane. We really need you. Not a stuntwoman on the continent."

I laughed nonchalantly and said, "I'm happy to be here. It was a long journey and I'm exhausted. See you tomorrow. Oh, by the way, when are we shooting the scene with the snake?"

"Oh, we shot that last week with the snake handler's wife. What's the matter? Are you afraid of snakes?"

He looked at me sideways.

"Of course not," I assured him. "I love the slimy little creatures."

I spun around and almost jumped for joy. *Woo-hoo!* I could relax and enjoy my job. Thanks be to God the snake ordeal was behind me. Without my participation!

When I'd accepted Don's invitation to work in South Africa, I made the best decision I could with the information available to me. And yet there were several factors over which I had no control. I *wanted* Sean to beg me to stay and make a baby. But that wasn't something over which I had any control. Conversely, I wanted to *not* be required to encounter any creatures that slithered on the ground and could wrap themselves around my body and choke me to death. But that was also outside of my control.

As you pursue your dream, there will be elements of it over which you'll have control. You can focus on your vision of success. You can rehearse what you need to do so that you're ready when you hear "action." You can even armor up with whatever's in your particular Red Bag of Courage! But there will also be elements of the dream that's in your heart over which you will have little or no control. Sometimes others will call the shots. You must make the best choice you can and then make the most of that choice.

Port St. Johns is a small coastal town known as the "Jewel of the Wild Coast." The area is called the Wild Coast for its ship-crushing waves. I had to sign a deal memo promising to stay out of the ocean: no swimming, surfing, or frolicking in the water due to the fierce waves and the hungry sharks. I was happy to oblige. Nearby, the massive Umzimvubu River beckoned as a playground for canoeing and fishing. The natural beauty of the jungle tapering into white sandy beaches with prehistoric rock formations and mesmerizing sunsets took my breath away.

Although South Africa didn't have stunt *women*, the producers were able to round up some stunt*men*. The sixteen young studly stuntmen were eager to meet the famous blond stuntwoman from Los Angeles. When I jumped out of the kombi on the set, the gang of guys rushed over to meet me, each one shoving the other out of the way to welcome me to their unique part of the world.

One blond, blue-eyed, hunky, local stuntman named Craig Ginsberg spoke softly to me and said, "I'll be your guide." Throughout the shoot he took it upon himself to watch out for me. Craig had an intriguing accent, tanned face, devilish smile, and chiseled muscles protruding from his tight black T-shirt.

He explained, "The very first thing that you need to be aware of is the black mamba snake. The black mamba is one of the fastest snakes and grows up to fourteen feet long. Legend has it that if it bites you, you take six steps and you're dead!"

"I'll be sure to keep an eye out for the black mamba. Thanks a lot," I laughed. He had no idea about my fear of snakes!

16

Before We'd Met Jack Sparrow

We were all taken to the wardrobe department, which was housed in a trailer, and were outfitted in pirate outfits long before Jack Sparrow was even imagined. I had a tattered pair of khaki pants and a torn olive-green shirt with voluminous sleeves. A worn black vest and a belt of bullets slung across my chest topped off the outfit perfectly. Rugged black leather boots with straps and spurs adorned my feet, and I was off to the hair department housed in another small trailer. A wig with long black stringy hair was anchored to my head with a red bandanna tied around my forehead.

The makeup lady darkened my eyebrows and lined my blue eyes with coal eyeliner. Black soot smudges decorated my face, and, for the final touch, a crew member handed me a vintage rifle. I was poised and ready for action!

Standing alongside other stuntmen who were dressed in similar pirate gear, we gathered for a meeting with the stunt coordinator,

Don Pike, and the director, Steve Carver. It was a night shot, and the jungle noises echoed between the director's words. Sounds of birds cawing and monkeys screaming rang in the thickness of the night air.

Steve explained, "You guys will be patrolling your hut here on the Umzimvubu River. You will be marching back and forth on the deck looking for pirate thieves who might be attacking you at any moment and trying to overtake you. Your hut is surrounded by weapons and enough gunpowder to blow any intruders to kingdom come. We will be shooting the master shot all leading up to the final shot when an attacking pirate ship enters your view. The pirate ship will then launch a bomb that directly hits your hut, and a massive explosion will occur hurling bodies into the cold, black Umzimvubu."

I looked around at the stunt guys. Some were shaking their heads and others backing away.

After Steve's description, Don Pike asked, "Who wants to be on the deck?"

I immediately shot my hand up. I wanted to be in the height of the action. I wanted to show those guys that I wasn't a wimp, and besides, being in the "hot seat," the most dangerous place, meant that I would get a bigger stunt adjustment that translated into major bucks.

Gary Pike, Don's brother, was in as well as two other South African stuntmen. In preparation, we walked around the drums of explosives that the special effects guy—who was missing a finger—had carefully set up. He described the nitro, which we are not allowed to use in the US, along with the assorted sizes of the gunpowder containers and charges setup. Having studied explosives for my pyrotechnic license, I knew this one would be a bell ringer! He explained to us the sequence of the explosions and spelled out the critical timing.

He said, "There will be three small explosions with fire and smoke, then a beat, and then the biggie will blow! You need to be facing away from the flying debris and be ready to get thrown into the river by the concussion of the blast."

My throat tightened, my lips got dry, and I thought, "Why the hell did I volunteer for this?" Quickly, I began to visualize the perfect outcome and know in my mind that it was going to be okay. I visualized me landing safely in the water and swimming to shore.

Don grabbed my arm and pulled me aside and said, "Are you ready to do this? You can back out now."

Laughing, I assured him, "Born ready!"

I couldn't back out now, nor did I want to.

Back in my dressing room, I put on my wet suit vest under my shirt to help with buoyancy. After all, the clothes would be wet and heavy. I said some prayers and asked God to keep us all safe and get me through the stunt unscathed. Confident, I marched to the set focused on a successful outcome. Surveying the shoreline for large rocks and tree limbs that might hinder my escape from the river, I planned my route.

Craig, my protector, came along and said, "Diane I brought this rope for you. I'm going to hide it behind this tree. If I see you are in trouble, I'll throw you the rope and you grab on, okay?"

"Thanks for looking out for me Craig, you are an angel," I smiled and kept focused on my task at hand.

After pausing to do some deep breathing, I was ready. It was about four o'clock in the morning, and I was tired and anxious to get the explosions behind me. Waiting for the big moment is always the hardest part. It's important to remain cool and calm while the tension on the set is mounting on all sides.

At the last minute, the weapons man asked me, "Can you please remember to throw your rifle down before the blast so you won't lose it in the water? Every rifle must be accounted for."

I smiled and nodded *yes* while thinking that it was the last thing I was going to worry about. I was much more concerned about my head being blown off. Gary Pike was standing next to me, and we made a pact to watch out for one another. I trusted him completely and he knew I always had his back.

During the rehearsal, we marched back and forth on the wooden slat deck, suspended by thick maritime ropes. Peering out over the black ominous river, we scanned the horizon for intruders.

The director kept reminding us on the bullhorn, "There will be three small explosions with fire and smoke and then on the count of three the big bomb is going to blow!"

The cameramen, the director, and all of the crew were hundreds of feet away tucked behind a barrage of trees. They weren't taking any chances of getting hit with flying debris. My gang and I were the ones in the hotseat.

My blood was rushing, and the butterflies were swarming in the pit of my stomach.

Steve yelled, "OK, we're ready to roll. Go hot on the bombs! Camera's rolling!"

As I peered out over the water, I saw a huge black snake swimming toward the spot where I had anticipated landing. I instantly recognized it as a Black Mamba.

"Hold the roll!" I screamed. "Hold the roll!"

"Hold the roll!" Steve yelled. "What it is Diane?"

I reported, "There's a huge snake swimming toward me in the water."

The special effects guys got in a dingy and chased the snake downstream with a torch. I was happy for that and somewhat relieved, but I wondered where its mother and father and the rest of the snake family were lurking. Once again, I had to focus and overcome my fear.

"We are ready to roll again," Steve yelled. "Bombs hot, rolling cameras, and action!"

As I marched on the wobbly deck, my body was a massive tingling of nerves. Smelling smoke, I heard the sizzling sound of the explosive cord and then the first *boom,* then there was more smoke and two quick *boom, booms* then a beat, a beat, a beat and I'm thinking where is the big one . . .

KABOOM!

The concussion knocked me head over heels flying through the air. I came down hard on my back in the middle of the river. Hitting the water was like hitting pavement. With the wind knocked out of me, my clothes were wet and heavy, and I was sinking fast. I began swimming like mad toward the shore nearly hitting shards of burning timbers. Dragging myself onto the bank, exhausted, I looked back to see where Gary was. Spotting him in the water, I saw him struggling and gasping for breath.

Running to get the hidden rope, I threw it to him and yelled, "Gary, Gary grab the rope, grab the rope!"

He fumbled for it a few times and then he finally got hold of it.

"Hang on Gary," I assured him, "I got you."

I dragged him as hard as I could, pulling and pulling, slipping and sliding, until he reached the shore. Huffing and puffing, he was completely spent.

"Thanks, man," he gushed. "You saved my ass. I couldn't make it."

We just held each other and cried. I was so thankful that we made it out safely.

Finally, the director yelled over the bullhorn, "Cut! That was fucking marvelous!"

That explosion was by far the biggest that I'd ever experienced. It was such an adrenaline rush that Gary and I spent hours talking well into the morning about life and the future. It wasn't easy to come down from a high like that. Gary, a truly wonderful sweetheart of a guy, and I now shared a special bond.

One bit of African wisdom that's made its way around the globe is, "It takes a village to raise a child." The sentiment is that a child thrives when there are many who care for that child. I've certainly found that insight to be true throughout my career. While some sectors of the industry can feel like "every man for himself," I've much preferred working in spaces of mutual care. Thinking of my safety, Craig brought me a rope to be hidden away in case I'd need it. And in the end, I was able to share it with Gary when he was in need. I know for a fact that sets are safer when we're looking out for one another, and I think it's fair to say that we all achieve more when we practice a spirit of generosity and care for others. While that spirit of community might look a variety of ways in the space you inhabit, I encourage you to keep your eyes open for how you can be useful to someone else. If you are working on the set, look for ways you can lend a hand even if it's not your department. Working together for the good of all is the win.

17

Trouble on Set

One beautiful early morning I arrived on the set to find a small village had been erected in a clearing of the dense jungle. The village consisted of several small rondavels that were white mud huts with thatched roofs. There were hundreds of native Xhosas—one of the Bantu peoples' ethnic groups—dressed in costumes made of reeds. Their dark skin was adorned with brilliant white and red body paint, and they talked in a unique language made of clicking noises.

The "x" in Xhosa is represented by a click like the noise we make to urge a horse to advance forward. There was a myriad of clicking sounds surrounding me, almost like a symphony of crickets. There were small burning firepits scattered around with natives huddled around them swaying and humming to an African beat. It was enchanting and mesmerizing.

The director, Steve Carver, and Don Pike approached me as I watched in awe of the native camaraderie.

Steve explained, "Diane, in this scene we have Donald Pleasance being captured by the natives. The natives don't understand English, and the translator is having a tough time explaining in 'clicks' what I want to happen."

Just then, the prop guy called me and I was given a large club that looked like a dinosaur bone. The top of the club had a foam rubber cap on it, painted to look like a giant bone. I could beat Donald Pleasance over the head with this and avoid knocking him out for real. I was armed and ready. I even started clicking to get into character, but I had no idea what my clicks meant. I was given a tiny top made of feathers that barely covered my breasts and a skimpy skirt made of colorful leaves and reeds.

I had to be barefoot, so my tender feet stung as I made my debut on the rough jungle floor. I heard drums beating and saw a group of natives dancing, so I joined in with them, swaying my hips, rotating my shoulders, and chanting a haunting melody. I inhaled the sweet smell of marijuana wafting through the air and noticed a group of natives smoking an enormous fat joint rolled in newspaper. I wanted to sashay over and try a hit, but I was working, and it would have to wait until later.

Steve explained, "I want you all to mingle with the natives and when the warrior chief blows his horn, signaling that intruders are approaching, Diane, I want you to grab your club, charge Donald, grab him, and beat him over the head with the club until he falls. Then Craig and Joe will drag him back to the warrior chief."

We all nodded and gave a thumbs-up. I walked over and introduced myself to Donald, a small bald-headed old man, who was looking extremely nervous. Extending my weapon, I let him feel the top of the club which was made of soft foam rubber. I told him that I would look and act very aggressive, but I would not hurt him. I gave him a pair of kneepads so when he fell, he could go to his knees and gently collapse. He seemed relieved that I could speak English and that I was a trained stuntwoman.

There were hundreds of natives milling around. Some were dancing, and I joined them in their rhythmic movements to the sound of the drumbeats. I was really getting into the energetic vibe when Steve yelled, "Camera's rolling, and action!" When I heard the warrior chief blow the cow horn, I ran as fast as I could, dodging natives, club in hand, and grabbed Donald by the neck and began beating him over the head. He looked terrified and quickly fell to the ground. Craig and Joe dragged him away as I returned to dance around with joy alongside my native friends. We shot this scene over and over again for five or six hours with different camera angles and various close-ups. Between takes, I would hang out with the stunt guys and listen to their harrowing tales of stunt life in South Africa. And they all wanted the details of what it was like working stunts in Hollywood.

Life in Port St. Johns was always an adventure for me. On my days off, I would hike in the jungle with a few of the stunt guys. Craig was always in the pack, and I'd feel him quietly observing me while all the others tried to show off by climbing trees or jumping huge ravines. The other guys were usually trying to test my courage and bravery, challenging me to do silly daredevil acts like walking across a log suspended over a deep gully. Sometimes, I would join in and show them I could do anything they could, and other times I would huddle with Craig and find a way to lose them. I didn't want to be constantly tested, and I certainly didn't want to get hurt on my time off.

On one particularly cloudless day under the incredible rich, indigo South African sky, Craig and I climbed up a narrow rocky path on the side of a steep mountain. We were exhausted and found a tiny landing to rest on. He asked me about my life in LA, and I told him that I was married, explaining that I really wanted a baby, but that my husband was doing nothing that the doctor suggested to make that a reality.

Craig laughed and said, "Guess he doesn't want a baby as much as you do."

He was right on with that insight.

Craig told me about his last love and said that she did not want him to be a stuntman, so he had to say goodbye. He kissed my forehead, grabbed my hand, and helped me up.

"You are here for a reason," he said. "Let me help you enjoy your time in my country. There is an incredible horseback safari in the Zulu bush that I'd love to take you on when the filming is done. Think about it, okay?"

I was comforted and thrilled to have Craig as my buddy in this faraway land.

Once a week, on Sunday, I received a phone call from Sean. We usually talked for only a few minutes. The rates were expensive, and we mostly talked about business: the house, the cars, the taxes, and meaningless dialogue followed by the obligatory "I-miss-yous." The truth was that I really did not miss him much at all. I inwardly resented the fact that he so willingly sent me on my way to make money instead of insisting I stay home to make a baby. Granted, each day I was enjoying all the attention and admiration from the stunt guys and performing the myriad of stunts that came my way. But the nights were lonely. I had an extremely basic, sterile room with white walls and a small twin bed with a mattress that had springs that jabbed me in my back as I turned over. There was a single stark-white lightbulb hanging from the ceiling in the middle of the room. I got so tired of staring at that lonely lightbulb that I used my creativity to make a chandelier! One evening, I got some colored cellophane and glue from the lighting department and constructed an amazing chandelier-like fixture to adorn the lonely bulb. I also bought a tiny transistor radio that had only one station on it. The music was a primal African beat that I was beginning to really enjoy. It always made me feel like moving my hips and dancing. I was so proud of my creation that I invited Gary over to see it. He thought I was going nuts.

There were only two restaurants at the hotel for dinner and no other restaurants nearby. The large restaurant was a cafeteria, and the food was unusual to say the least. We ate there most evenings, grabbing our trays and sliding down the line of strange dishes resembling monkey tails and pigs' feet. The food was very inexpensive and bland with a gritty type of pasty pasta that stuck to the roof of your mouth like hot tar. Most evenings all the stunt guys would have dinner with me, and we would have food fights and behave like children. Then we would go to the bar and drink like men! They enjoyed buying drinks for me and trying to get me drunk. I had an amazing capacity to down liquor and not get loaded, so I would usually be the last one standing and slip off to my hotel room. Occasionally, I would go to the fine dining room with Don, his wife Leslie, and his brother Gary. Gary liked me a lot, but I liked him only as a brother. He knew and respected that and my marriage as well. We enjoyed delicious steaks and fine South African wine as we discussed the upcoming action scenes. We also talked a lot about Steve, the director, who was becoming a tyrant. It was a difficult shoot with so many natives, and the equipment was not up to par. Also, those with any addictions could not get their medicine of choice in this faraway land. We joked that the place was called the "Betty Ford Clinic."

Tension was mounting between Don and Steve. Late one night when we were shooting a complicated scene, Steve screamed at Don and Don told him to fuck off. Don was considering quitting.

I didn't want him to quit because I didn't want to go home yet. Don and Gary were also getting jealous of the attention I was showing to Craig. Between takes, Craig and I would sit and talk about our dreams and goals. We were forming a wonderful friendship. One day, Don fired Craig for no apparent reason. Craig came to my trailer to say goodbye, and I couldn't believe he was leaving. I was devastated.

I said, "I'm so deeply sorry. This is my fault for spending too much time with you."

He assured me that it was not my fault. That it was meant to be.

And he smiled and reminded me, "Think about the Zulu bush safari. I'll be your guide."

18

Do the Right Thing

The next morning, I climbed into the kombi. Craig usually sat next to me. I was missing him already. His friend Steve plopped down next to me and smelled like he needed a shower.

"Good morning, Miss Diane," he chimed. "Too bad about my mate Craig."

I really did not feel like talking about it, so I just nodded and stared out the window. I still had another month to go, and losing my buddy made me feel all alone again. I remembered the safari offer and dreamed of riding through the bush dodging elephants and hyenas. We arrived at our location where hundreds of wildebeests were roaming. I just loved looking at these strange creatures with giant shaggy heads and twisted horns. They had bodies almost like horses but had abbreviated sloping shoulders and could run like the wind.

In the distance was an enormous Sikorsky helicopter sitting in waiting. The chopper was so huge it resembled a blimp. I wondered if the maintenance and safety records were kept strictly up to date like they are required to do in America. I hoped they were! When we all gathered for our safety meeting with the director, he explained that we all would be riding in the Sikorsky as it dive-bombed toward the bridge where the camera crew would be shooting. The helicopter would be doing some dangerous dives, and we were to be looking out the windows. I thought, *Why aren't they just putting dummies in the seats?* Then I realized that we were in the middle of nowhere and had no dummies. Just as I hated riding as a passenger in a sports car during a stunt, I felt the same way about not being in control in a helicopter. But I hopped on board and took a seat in the back, as if that would ensure my safety if that flying bumblebee crashed. The eight stunt guys were laughing and pushing each other around while I was noticing the pilot. He looked way too young to possibly know what he was doing. Moments before we were ready to take off, the pilot's pager went off. As he immediately exited the chopper without saying a word, we were told to remain seated. About an hour later, another pilot showed up who looked a lot more mature with graying sideburns and a confident stride. When we asked him what happened to the other pilot, he reported that he worked for an important government official and when he received calls, he was required to immediately report for duty. I felt more comfortable with our new commander, Robert, until I noticed him reading the manual for the aircraft!

I said, "Steve, this guy is reading the frigging manual! I bet he's never flown this clumsy thing."

He laughed and said, "Relax and enjoy the ride."

As the helicopter took off, all the wildebeests went running like a herd of charging buffalo. It was an incredible sight, such beauty in motion. I said some prayers and asked God to keep us safe. Just then the pilot swooped down toward the bridge, and I saw the cameramen hit the deck! *Oh my God, we are going to crash.* At the very last possible second the pilot pulled up on the controls and we skimmed over the cameras and headed toward the bright blue sky. There was silence in the aircraft. Glancing at one another, I knew we were all thinking the same thing: *hope we don't have to do that again!* Being a passenger in a situation like that is insane. And yet there I was, along for the ride, unable to scream, "Get me out of here!" Deep down inside, though, I admit that the thrill that was irreplaceable. This was my dream, living for the thrill and loving it.

As the extreme dives continued all afternoon on several different bridges, I continued thinking positive thoughts and remained calm at every plunge. After a while it was almost like a roller coaster ride. When the pilot finally said he had to refuel I was delighted. My feet were never so happy to hit the ground. Don gave us all an extra $900 stunt adjustment which was well-earned—despite the fact that at the bar that evening, as we slammed down shots of crappy whiskey to settle our nerves, no one ever admitted to being terrified.

On some of my days off I would go hiking and canoeing with the guys. They were all like brothers to me and quite protective. I even found a place to shop in the jungle. The Pondo people created all types of beaded clothing and bracelets, and I bought colorful necklaces and beaded pants that I still have to this day!

Craig surprised me with a phone call one evening, and I told him that I decided to do the safari with him. After all, when would I ever be back this way again? As happy as I was for the confirmation, he explained that he would book the horseback safari for the day after I was scheduled to return to Johannesburg.

One week before filming was scheduled to end, we were shooting a night shot at about 4:30 a.m. with lots of explosives. It had been a long shoot and the director was getting edgy and tense, barking orders at the crew.

We were all standing around waiting to be told what our action was to be when Steve yelled at Don Pike in front of all of us.

"Don, what the fuck are you standing around for?" he bellowed. "We need to get this shot done before daybreak!"

Don walked off the set. *Should I follow him and walk off the set or do I stay and complete the shot?* I knew that one more week meant approximately another $4,000, and I had made a commitment to go on that safari with Craig. The date for the safari was set and if I quit the show, I would have to hang around Jo'burg for a week till safari time.

I decided to stay on the set that night, and in Don's absence, Steve put me in charge of all the guys. I explained the shot in detail to them and mapped out the choreography of who would run where as the bombs were exploding. We did several rehearsals to set the timing with the special effects team. When Steve called action, my ballet of men and bombs exploding was perfectly executed. Steve thanked me for staying and planning a great shot, and he asked me if I would complete the picture with him. I told him that I needed to talk to Don in the morning before I made that decision. That night I couldn't sleep as I wrestled over what to do. Don was an exceptionally good friend and we worked together a lot. I didn't want to jeopardize our special relationship.

Later that morning, on my way to breakfast, I walked past Don's room and saw his bags packed outside his door. I entered the cafeteria and slowly walked over to him.

"Don, do you want me to leave with you? I will if you want me to."

He grunted, "You can stay if you want to. It's up to you. I'm getting the hell out of here. I can't take another day with Steve."

"Don, I'm going on a safari when the movie ends," I explained, "and so I'd really like to stay."

"Okay . . . see you in LA," he muttered as he pushed his chair back from the table and hugged me goodbye.

That final week, the tension seemed to disappear and filming went smoothly. We had a blast running through the jungle, canoeing, and racing around in jeeps, doing pickup shots that we might have overlooked and shooting some extra footage for the film.

Saying goodbye on movie sets is never easy. Cast and crew have worked, played, laughed, and sometimes cried together for months with those who've become newfound family. And when working on a remote location like Port St. Johns, there is little contact with anyone else, especially at that time in the late eighties when the internet was still just a tiny seed about to explode. Film crews usually have a wrap party to celebrate the completion of the filming and to bid farewell to one another. While there were always hopes of working together again someday, I knew on this occasion that I would probably never see any of these stunt guys or crew again. It was highly unlikely that they would make it to Los Angeles, and it was doubtful that I would ever be sent to South Africa again. It had been one of those once-in-a-lifetime opportunities. I felt fortunate to have spent many exciting days and nights making the film, but now it was time to return to reality. My short excursion on the horseback safari with Craig would be the final icing on the cake.

Though I'd explained to Sean that I was staying four extra days to go on a horseback safari, he didn't seem to care one way or another. So, I was glad that I had agreed to go on the adventure.

I flew to Jo'burg and met Craig, who I was thrilled to see. We headed out for the Zulu bush, which was a several-hour trip by car. Laughing and talking about the filming on the ride, we arrived at the Bush Lodge in the heart of the KwaZulu-Natal, where we were greeted by our guide Gometi, a huge Black man who knew few English words.

Gometi led us to a cozy rondavel with a beautiful thatched roof. There were kerosene lanterns and no electricity. Animal skin rugs adorned the floor, and the sweet fragrance of honeysuckle was intoxicating. We heard distant sounds of hyenas laughing, birds chirping, and cheetahs roaring. After starting a fire for us outside in the pit for a *braai*, which is a type of South African barbecue, Gometi promised he would bring the horses at daybreak for our journey. That evening, a perfectly peaceful night in the dense jungle, Craig and I enjoyed a lovely dinner under the stars. I was happy and content to be in this wonderland with this unique man.

At daybreak, I heard horses whinnying. After drinking some coffee, we headed out for the adventure of a lifetime. Gometi was carrying a gun just in case an exotic animal wanted to try a little people meat. He told us that he scattered freshly killed chickens around to appease the hungry wild beasts. He explained that we should only speak in whispers as not to disturb or frighten the wildebeests, impalas, cheetahs, and giraffes who roamed in the bush. In the distance I spotted a giant giraffe running frantically in circles. We crept closer on horseback, and sadly noticed a newborn giraffe lying motionless in the tall grass. The cheetah who was roaming around the next bend would surely have a tasty breakfast very soon. Feeling bad for the mommy giraffe, I longed to console her. The ways of the bush are cruel and only the most fit survive.

We heard brilliantly colored birds tweeting and welcoming the morning and saw herds of wildebeests grazing in the fertile land. That morning I felt immeasurable joy. KwaZulu-Natal kindled my love of the animals in their habitat safely enjoying the fruits of the planet.

At midday, the three of us returned to the camp, as most of the animals would take a nap during the hottest part of the day. Gometi promised to return at sunset for another adventure into the wild. Craig and I hiked to an amazing waterfall and spent the afternoon talking about our hopes and dreams for the future and frolicking in the pools of glistening water.

As the sun set, a miraculous orange hue colored the bush. We mounted our horses and began searching for more incredible animals. I spotted a trio of rhinoceroses in the distance having dinner. The mother, the baby, and the father bull grazed peacefully. The beautiful moment left me speechless. We tiptoed closer and I gave my camera to Craig to take a photo of me with the rhino family. As he quickly snapped a shot, I heard the bull stomp his foot. His flared nostrils and an angry snort communicated clearly that I was to vacate. I slowly urged my horse in an about face and prayed that the rhino would not charge us. Gometi had instructed us that if a rhino charged us, we should run our horses zigzag because the rhinos have extremely poor eyesight. My heart was beating so fast as we slowly and carefully created some distance between us. The bull rhino was still staring and snorting but, thankfully, he decided not to charge us.

The next few days were full of adventure with the gorgeous animals of the bush roaming free. And at night we enjoyed wonderful barbecues under the stars. When it was time for me to get home, we packed our things and headed for the airport, both hoping that one day our paths would cross again. Though that was the last time I saw Craig, he made my journey to South Africa extra special. One that I will never forget.

When I was in South Africa, I knew my marriage was shaky. I longed for my husband to desire to create a family together. And yet nothing about Sean's behavior, before my trip or during it, signaled that he shared my wish. That was the piece of my story that wasn't entirely in my control.

What was in my control was how I thought. How I spoke. How I behaved. I would just have to wait and see what the future will hold for us. Two kids, two horses, two ponies, and a dog was my vision, and I clung to it dearly.

19

Coming Home to the USA

Retracing the route I'd traveled eight weeks earlier in reverse, my final flight at last touched down in Los Angeles. I was exhausted but eager to see my husband. When I spotted him at the airport, I rushed into his arms and he kissed me, but it felt strange, distant, cold. *Is it me? Or has the glue that once cemented our relationship evaporated?* He had a limo waiting outside, which seemed to show some effort, but I sensed no depth of feeling at all. As I excitedly talked about my adventures, Sean showed little interest. After a ride that seemed endless, I felt a cold chill between us as we walked into the house. Collapsing into bed, both keeping our distance, the awkward cool cloud I'd noticed followed us into the bedroom.

For the first few days after my return, I tried to get back into the rhythm of life in Simi Valley. Despite brutal jet lag, I focused on looking for my next job.

A few nights after my return, Sean announced, "We need to talk in the morning."

Curious, I suggested, "Let's talk now."

He replied bluntly, "I don't love you anymore. I'm leaving."

I was aware of some cracks in our foundation, but I felt we could work everything out and have a sweet, loving family.

He then added sharply, "I've been living a charade, pretending to be your loving husband."

The words cut like a knife, but I offered, "We can work it out, let's go for counseling."

Sean's reply was curt.

"I don't want to air my dirty laundry. I've made a decision."

And off he went to sleep in the guest bedroom. I was crushed, thinking about the baby that we, or should I say *I*, had been planning to have. It was a complete shock. I knew things weren't great, but I'd still been willing to work on our marriage.

"Divorce" wasn't in my vocabulary. At the altar I'd promised "till death do us part" in good times and bad, and I'd meant it. As a Catholic, I was committed to my marriage vows.

Wanting to reconcile, I sought out Sean in the guest room. When I tried to lie down beside him, he spit out just two ugly words.

"Get out." My heart was broken. This couldn't be happening.

In the morning, Sean was gone.

I soon discovered that he was "doing" his secretary, Kelly, who had two kids and had left her husband a few months before. She was the one that night at the party who kept staring at him. I sensed trouble with her, and I was right. She was a home-wrecker and Sean was her prey.

The hurt sliced a deep wound in my heart, but with God by my side, I gathered the strength to continue. Knowing that I was strong, I believed that someday I'd find happiness again. But I cried every time I thought of the baby I so desperately wanted to have. At thirty-seven, I feared I would likely never have the chance again. At the time, I thought that it was a wicked thing for Sean to do to me, but looking back, it was a blessing. I suspect he would have been a rotten father, just like his father had been to him.

I wanted to keep the house, and per the terms of our settlement, I had to give Sean $50,000 to buy him out. I wrote him a farewell note reading, "Time is the coin of our lives, thanks for not wasting any more of my time. Take this $50,000 and shove it." Though I'd wanted to preserve my marriage and was willing to make sacrifices to do it, I was truly glad he was gone. A deceitful man is worse than no man at all.

Dana, my best friend, helped through this difficult time. She was an excellent stuntwoman, and we rode horses and motorcycles together. We went skiing and talked for hours in my hot tub. Her kindness and caring helped ease the agony of my divorce. We attended church together, and I even became her godmother.

The very best way to recover from my heartbreak was to keep working and get some therapy! Around that same time, I was called to work on the movie *Blue Sky* to double Jessica Lange who I'd doubled on *King Kong* quite a few years earlier. I flew into El Paso, Texas on a crisp, beautiful sunny morning. As I exited the aircraft, I spotted a tall, crusty-looking cowboy holding a sign with my name on it.

We exchanged pleasantries and he informed me, "Tommy wants to see you at the ranch."

"Tommy" was Tommy Lee Jones. I knew we'd be using his horses for the filming. Fortunately, I was dressed for the occasion in tight jeans, cowboy boots, fitted denim shirt, and a sexy leather belt. I hopped out of the van at the ranch and saw Tommy walking toward me with two beautiful horses. Looking stern, he was ready for business.

I smiled and said, "Hi, I'm Diane Peterson."

He nodded, as if he knew that already, stared at me and growled, "Can you ride?"

"Yes, sir." I confidently replied.

He was so serious that for a moment I wanted to approach the horse on the wrong side and attempt to mount up, just for laughs. My better judgment prevailed, and I figured that Tommy probably would not find the humor in that situation at all! We jumped on our horses, and he took off in a full gallop. I followed right on his heels and had my steed in complete control. He looked back and finally smiled at me. Once I got that nod of approval, I was good to go. All those years of riding lessons once again paid off.

One of the stunts in the movie required me to gallop a horse in the desert with a helicopter chasing me. That was all well and fine with me, except the horse had never been near a helicopter before! Also, the helicopter would be chasing us and flying extremely close overhead. The loud noise coupled with the ominous shadows that the rotating blades cast on the desert floor threw the horse into a frenzy. As he kept trying to jump over the shadows, I had to squeeze him tight with my knees and urge him on during the exciting, bumpy gallop. The sand was blowing volumes of dust in our eyes, and as I reached my mark, an enormous atomic bomb explosion went off. My horse stood straight up and reeled around and around in a circle on his hind legs.

Holding on for dear life I coaxed, "Easy, big boy, easy."

The explosion was much bigger than I had expected. They often are. I felt the intense heat on my face and neck, and my ears were ringing despite the ear plugs I had inserted before the stunt. My throat was parched from the desert sand as I calmed my nervous horse.

Continuing to pet his neck, I gently soothed, "It's okay, boy, settle down."

Just then I heard the director yell over the loudspeaker, "That's a print."

I was delighted that I didn't have to repeat the stunt, and I'm sure the horse was too!

In another scene, Jessica's husband and boyfriend are arguing, and she attempts to get between them to stop the fight. That's where I stepped in and got pushed through a rather large window. (Something about me and windows—I was always busting through them! This time I didn't drag my hands!)

I also did a few driving sequences in an old station wagon. In one scene, I disrupted a parade by driving right through it. That was exhilarating for me and the kids who were riding with me.

When Jessica won an Academy Award for Best Actress for that movie, I felt happy and proud to think that I did my part to make that happen.

It wasn't long before I was working quite a bit on a television series in Denver called *Father Dowling Mysteries*. I was doubling Tracy Nelson, the daughter of Ricky Nelson, who was a sixties singing star. Tracy was thin as a twig, so I had to buckle down and starve myself to keep the job. Even though she was playing a nun and I'd have to run around in a nun's habit, when I showed up on the set, I needed to look very thin. I was in tip-top shape, but she was extremely slender. Because I was still upset about the divorce and didn't feel much like eating anyway, it really wasn't that much of a problem.

Working in Denver, which I loved, was a welcome change from Los Angeles, and it took my mind off the divorce. At the time, I was trying to decide whether I was going to stay in my house in Simi Valley or move back to Marina Del Rey. Since I first moved to Marina Del Rey when I arrived in LA, it had felt always like another home to me. As I looked at condos in the marina, I couldn't justify giving up my one-acre property on the mountaintop, with a beautiful home and a gorgeous waterfall pool, for a two-bedroom condo that cost practically the same amount. Everyone was telling me not to make any quick decisions in the first year after the divorce, which I agreed was good advice. So, I decided to stay at Rancho de la Estrella (Ranch of the Star), the name I'd given my home, even though it was a huge expense and a ton of maintenance for only one person to handle. I was grateful for the work on *Father Dowling Mysteries* because not only would I receive my checks for the immediate work, but I would get residuals for reruns for years to come if the show was a hit. And it was a big hit!

Because Tracy wasn't very athletic, I got to do many stunts that were fun and easy for me because she didn't care to do them. I hung from a moving conveyor belt in a dry cleaning store! Climbed over high cyclone fences! I had a blast! The hardest part of the gig was staying super thin after my appetite returned. This time it took a bit more effort to watch the carbs, and I had to eat like a bird.

I did a lot of stunt driving for Tracy in a big old station wagon, spinning and throwing slides all over town on the icy, snowy streets. In one episode, I was chasing the bad guys with three cop cars following me. Father Dowling's stunt double, Bob, and I had just rescued a baby from the bad guys, and we had a fake stunt baby doll in the car with us. On the last take, I talked Bob into throwing the baby out the window as we raced past the camera. Everyone had a huge laugh about that at the end of that day!

Running around in a nun's outfit makes for a lot of hilarious stories. One freezing cold day, we were about to begin filming outside a strip club. The honey wagons, which are dressing rooms with toilets in them, had not arrived yet and I needed to use one. So, I walked into the strip joint dressed as a nun.

The stunned guy at the front desk cleared his throat and said, "May I help you sister?"

I looked at him deadpan and said, "Yeah, I need a job!"

His mouth dropped as I began to laugh and then explained our shooting of the television series outside.

"Wow, I thought you were a stripping nun," he howled. "Never saw one of those!"

I had an enormous suite at the Embassy Suites in Denver with maid service, room service, gym, and everything I could possibly want, except *love*. Dating was weird after being with Sean for ten years.

Usually, when I first met a man who wasn't in the film business and told them that I was stuntwoman, they would immediately chuckle and say, "Ha! What kind of stunts do you do?"

Their thoughts usually revolved around me swinging from a chandelier naked over their bed.

Though I didn't have that one special someone, I had a lot of set "buddies" on *Father Dowling Mysteries*. The assistant directors, stunt guys, wardrobe, and makeup ladies would all hang out at the bar in the hotel after work and then go out dancing. Life was full of adventures that kept my mind busy and not rehashing what went wrong in my marriage. After all, I knew what went wrong: *I married the wrong guy.*

In one episode, I actually got to operate a train! When a runaway train was taken hostage by a bad guy, I climbed into the speeding locomotive and whacked the bad guy in the head with a two-by-four before taking control of the train. How fun it was to learn how to operate the train and get paid big bucks for that, too! The huge locomotive sounded like a grumbling monster, and the braking distance was remarkedly massive. There were no sudden stops with that big monster.

On another episode, I got to drive a huge farm tractor with my habit flying in the cold, crisp Denver air. Because my Aunt Mary had a dairy farm when I was growing up, I definitely had some early tractor experience. Driving anything and everything was really born in my DNA.

One day, the stunt coordinator, Bob Bralver, asked me if I could drive an 18-wheeler. I didn't hesitate for a second.

"You bet I can. My dad had a trucking company and taught me handle an 18-wheeler." I bragged, "I can even throw one sideways if you need me to!"

I thought of the day my dad taught me to back the 18-wheeler in on the blind side into a parking space. We were in a huge vacant lot, and he had an old water heater and some large orange cones as markers. I can't tell you how many times I smashed into that water heater and knocked it over. I would cringe, and my dad would just jump out of the truck, right the water heater, and patiently tell me to have another shot at it. He made learning fun, and there was never any pressure. I had a forty-foot trailer attached to the tractor, so it took quite a bit of maneuvering to get the truck parked in place without hitting any of the obstacles. My practice paid off because when I went to get my license, I sailed smoothly through all the driving tests including backing in on the blind side. My dad was proudly watching with a huge grin on his face. I did my daddy proud, once again. No matter how many gears I'd grind, he loved teaching me to drive the big rigs. Because he always had a sense of humor about it, we had some unforgettable great times in and out of the truck.

One day, I was learning to downshift and then turn up a tight uphill ramp, and I missed the shift. The gears are synchronized so missing a shift makes it hard to find the correct next gear. I was so frustrated that I just wanted to pull over and quit.

My dad calmly said, "Take it easy and don't push the panic button. Just put it in neutral and start over."

My dad's sage advice is wisdom that has served me well over the years. When we get frustrated, it's natural to want to abdicate the driver's seat. To pull over and quit. But we only hurt ourselves if we believe the only two options available to us are succeeding with ease or throwing in the towel. My dad reminded me of that third option: put it in neutral and start over.

As you pursue your dream, you can expect to encounter obstacles. At some point you'll miss the shift on a tight uphill ramp. But when you do, you don't have to quit. The other option is that you pause, breathe, put it in neutral, and start over. Maybe you're feeling stuck today. And maybe it's time to release the panic button, get your bearings, and start over. Sometimes you'll be able to make that adjustment on your own, and other times you can seek the support of your copilot. Pause. Breathe. Shift to neutral. Start again.

The *Father Dowling* coordinator gave me my chance to show my ability wheeling the semi-trailer around the maze of obstacles they set for me. I was still doubling Tracy, but this time she was going undercover as a truck driver. So goodbye nun's habit! I climbed into the truck with my blue jeans, denim jacket, and ball cap, pushed in the clutch, revved the engine, and waited for action. On action, I floored the gas and smoothly shifted gears as I wheeled the enormous truck between nondescript traffic, driven by other stunt drivers, and around tight corners. I was confident and having the time of my life! Although one take was all we needed to get the shot, I just wanted to keep driving all day.

The director marveled, "Wow! Diane, where did you learn to drive like that?"

I proudly boasted, "My daddy taught me."

When the episode ended, I flew home to an empty house on the hill where I sat in my hot tub staring at the sky and wondering if I'd ever meet someone special again. It was tough making house payments by myself and also paying the gardener, pool guy, taxes, and so on. No sooner would a check come in than it would fly right out of my hands. Plus, I was lonely in my castle on the hill.

20

New Possibilities, New Beginnings

The unexpected blessing of the divorce that I did not want was that it afforded me precious time to spend with my beloved father in New Jersey. Sadly, my mother was by then wheelchair-bound, unable to leave the house. While it was incredibly sad to see my mom unable to join in the fun, my dad had a caregiver to look after my mom while we would go golfing.

My dad was such a wonderful man with a wealth of inner joy that no outer circumstances could invade. He had always wanted to teach me to golf, but I would laugh and say, "Golf is for old people, Dad." But now I was older and had the time and patience to learn how to play. Even though I was living in Simi Valley, California, and my dad lived in Elmwood Park, New Jersey, it didn't stop our lessons. Between jobs, I would fly to New Jersey and spend a week or so driving the 18-wheeler with my dad and practicing golf every chance we got.

Boy, was I terrible at golf! I blamed my inability to master the swing on my years of playing softball. I had that swing down pat! My father was incredibly patient as I would hack away at the tiny golf ball. When we began our lessons, I wondered how anyone could think that it was fun. But gradually I began to relax, hit the ball, and enjoy the moment. Being with my dad in a beautiful setting, having him teach me to play a game he loved, was so special. Little by little, I made small increments of progress and learned to keep my head down and my eye on the ball. The score never mattered to us.

My dad also traveled west to be with me. He loved the sunshine and would fly out to California and spend some time with me every chance he could. When I'd bought my home in Simi Valley, he'd really wanted to move to California. He had his eye on a model home just down the street that was completely furnished with a cute little barn behind it. I knew he imagined taking care of my horses and probably my kids, too. That would have been so sweet for all of us. My mother, though, would have no part in moving to California. She found change difficult to handle. Plus, my dad had built her dream house for her in New Jersey and she loved the home so much.

On one trip, my dad and I journeyed to Pebble Beach. I was particularly nervous about playing this famous course. We had a beautiful drive up the coast, and when we checked into The Lodge at Pebble Beach, the message light was blinking on the phone. *Who would be calling us?* Lo and behold, it was Teddy's answering service. When I phoned them, they said I had a call for a job. I told them that no job was as important as golfing Pebble Beach with my dad. I never turned down jobs, but this time my dad was my priority.

The next day we got paired up with a nice older couple and I quickly sized up the female competition. Even in golf, I was competitive. I teed up on hole number one in front of a small crowd that had gathered to watch. I focused on the tiny white ball and kept my head down. *Whack!* Right down the middle of the fairway. I could see the glee in my father's eyes. When the other lady teed off and shanked it badly, I became confident that I could beat her.

On another hole, a giant precipice jutted out over the ocean. A player had to execute a shot from one cliff to another or watch her ball land in the ocean below. The other lady immediately said that she was going to the drop zone on the other side. She was too chicken to even try to hit a ball over the chasm.

I announced, "I'm going to go for it."

Stepping up to the tee box, addressing my ball, I concentrated on launching it to the other side successfully. Just like I mentally rehearsed my stunts. *Whack!* My ball sailed through the air, over the perilous ocean below, and landed safely on the edge of the cliff. Jumping up and down, my dad embraced me in a big bear hug. Then we hopped in our cart and laughed secretly on our victory ride. Priceless memories like that are forever etched in my mind.

My dad had never been to Hawaii, and on another occasion, we took a trip to Maui together. We golfed every day for a week! After my dad shot an amazing shot over a hill, we approached the green, but we couldn't see his ball.

I said, "Dad, it probably went in the hole."

We darted over to the hole and there it was. Two strokes on a par four: a big fat eagle! We danced around like little kids hooting and hollering.

We went to a pig roast, watched the hula dancers, ate macadamia nuts, and golfed for hours on end every day. We talked about everything under the sun when we golfed and really had some beautiful one-on-one time for which I'll always be grateful.

A few months later, we went to Bermuda where we discovered pink sand beaches, majestic perfectly groomed golf courses, English manors, and a whole new world for the two of us to explore. The morning after our arrival, we were paired up with a lovely older gentleman whose wife met us and announced she was going to have her hair done and read while her husband golfed. Although my dad longed to be able to share trips like that with my mom, she was in no shape to travel. He had me to enjoy his passion for golf, and I had the time to enjoy my dad with no jealous husband around. I cherish those days.

My split from Sean also made room for me to reconnect with friends. When my stuntwoman friend, Donna Garret, had called me one day to ask if I wanted to go skiing in Aspen, I'd gladly agreed. Since my divorce, I'd embarked on a whirlwind of dating and was weary of the dating game, so I was happy to get away with Donna. After skiing in Aspen like maniacs for a few days, we were starting to drag. So, we decided to have an extra cup of coffee at the hotel one morning before we hopped on the bus to Snowmass. Caffeinated, we marched through the white fluffy snow and waited for the bus. I was decked out in an all-white form-fitting ski suit, sporting a glowing tan, and my long blond hair flew in the breeze as I boarded the crowded bus that would shuttle us to the mountain. I spotted a seat near the back and sat down next to a handsome guy who was smiling.

He queried, "Are you ready for a great day of skiing?"

Playfully, I volleyed back with, "I was born ready."

I quickly learned that the stranger with the beautiful blue eyes and inviting smile was Jack from Plano, Texas.

I laughed, asking, "Where the heck is that?"

When he explained that it was near Dallas and that he was a dentist, I suddenly hoped that I'd remembered to floss that morning! Before I knew it, we arrived at our bus stop destination at Snowmass. Jack invited me to ski with him and his band of buddies. I told him that I didn't like to ski in crowds, but that I'd meet him at the end of the day in the bar at the base of the ski lift. Then Donna and I took off and covered the mountain trails all day.

When we were about to leave the ski area she said, "Let's catch that next bus back to the lodge."

I quickly replied, "I told that guy, Jack, that I'd meet him for a drink."

So, we entered the bar and there he was, smiling and waving, seemingly thrilled to see me. The band was playing loud rock and roll, and the party was just getting started. I ordered a Jack Daniels on the rocks, and before long, things were heating up. The band was deafening, so we had to lean in close to hear each other talk. Donna was busy talking to one of Jack's friends, Bob, another dentist from Dallas. Jack asked me to go to out to dinner that night, but I said that Donna and I had plans and I that I would go out with him the next night.

He said, "Good, that will give me time to plan the date."

Wow! I thought. *Here's a guy who actually plans dates!*

Later that night, Donna and I were waiting at the bar for our table in a trendy restaurant. I was wearing tight black jeans, furry snow boots, and a sexy red sweater. Jack walked in with his buddies and was quite surprised to see us there. We chatted briefly, and he sent a bottle of wine to our table later when we were having dinner. I thought it was a nice touch.

The next evening, I was sitting in the lobby of my hotel waiting for Jack to pick me up and a huge stretch woody limo arrived, and he jumped out of it! He looked super cute in a colorful silk shirt and buttery black leather jacket. Those blue eyes were burning brightly as he spotted me in my skintight black leather pants and coyote fur coat. He ushered me into the limo and the Red Hot Chili Peppers were playing, "Why Don't We Get Drunk and Screw?" We screamed and laughed at the lyrics, but I think he was hoping that sentiment would be realized that night.

Popping the champagne, he toasted to a fabulous night. Off we went to a romantic dinner in a tiny candlelit cabin. His blue eyes pierced my soul and melted my heart. We dished about us both growing up on the East Coast, me being from New Jersey, and he growing up on Long Island. We shared the yummy Chateaubriand for two and sipped bubbly French champagne. After talking for hours, until there was no one left in the restaurant but us, he surprised me by calling for the Ultimate Taxi to take us dancing. The Ultimate Taxi is a unique Aspen taxi driven by a crazy guy who has a disco ball on the inside roof of his cab and strobe lighting blinking a mile a minute. He handed us both 3D glasses, and after Jack told him that I was a stuntwoman, he began sliding his cab around corners in the snowy streets while playing a keyboard and singing! It was a wild and crazy ride and we laughed until we cried. We arrived at a nightclub and danced till we were dripping wet and the place was shutting down. Jack walked me home to my hotel in a flurry of giant snowflakes. The full moon was orange and shining ever so brightly as we lingered inside a tiny gazebo and kissed passionately—a kiss that left me wanting more. It was almost impossible to say goodnight.

He whispered in my ear, "Let's go to my hotel," as he kissed my neck and held me tight.

As tempting as it was, I managed to say, "The body says yes, but the mind says no. I just met you, I can't do that. I'm sorry."

I didn't want to be just another one-night stand to anyone. I was leaving Aspen the next day and I didn't want the night to end, but I knew I had to say goodnight. He said he understood and asked me to have lunch with him before I left for the airport.

I answered, "Yes, yes of course, I'd love to."

Then, walking hand in hand the rest of the way to my hotel in the gently falling snow, we shared one last deep passionate kiss and we sadly said goodnight.

In my early twenties, I never would have guessed that at the age of forty-two, I would be divorced. My life had not unfolded the way that I thought it might. And while I never would have chosen divorce, I was finally able to see how losing one thing can make room for another. If Sean hadn't left me, I likely wouldn't have carved out space for the precious time I'd been able to spend with my dad. I also wouldn't have taken time for a girls' trip with my friend where I accidentally met someone who seemed to adore me.

When we're in the midst of suffering, it's hard to imagine that anything good is awaiting us in the future we can't yet see. And yet sometimes losing what we so desperately wanted will make room for something else to flourish. In my case, Sean's absence created space for new seeds of possibility. And I was eager to see what might grow.

The next morning there was a knock on my door, and I opened it to find Jack holding a single rose. He was about five feet, ten inches tall with a strong, sturdy build, curly brown hair, striking blue eyes, and a very attractive air of self-confidence. He took me in his arms and kissed me as I felt this very special pure love pouring out of him and enveloping me. We held hands as we walked and drifted through the light powdered snow that had fallen the night before. He was holding a shopping bag with his other hand, and I asked him what was in it.

"It's for you, my love." Then he teased, "You can open it when we get to the restaurant."

The tiny, cozy French restaurant smelled like bubbling cheese on French onion soup. We were seated in a secluded booth tucked away in the back corner of the intimate café. He handed me a gift wrapped in pretty pink paper with a satiny, snow-white bow on top.

"Should I open it now?" I asked as he gently kissed my lips and nodded yes.

I carefully unwrapped the beautiful package and was pleasantly surprised to see a book titled *Love Stories of Famous Silver Screen Couples.*

"Read what I wrote," he proudly boasted.

His words were touching:

These are love stories of famous lovers and our story is about to unfold. I've never met anyone like you, and I will count the days until we can be together again. With love, Jack.

We both ordered the yummy onion soup and played with the strands of bubbling cheese, laughing, and feeding each other morsels of dark chocolate for dessert as we talked nonstop. Then he asked me to meet him in Sun Valley, Idaho for his next ski trip. I knew there was an undeniable spark there that I needed to explore. He had a horse-drawn carriage waiting for us as we exited the restaurant. How sweet was that? Climbing into the carriage, the horseman wrapped us in a soft fluffy blanket.

Snuggling tight, I knew we both wished for one more day to be together. The clippety-clop of the huge Belgian horse's feet rang like chimes in the wind as we traveled back to my hotel. Donna was waiting outside looking at her watch.

"Come on Diane," she urged, "we are going to miss the plane."

Jack held me tight and said, "See you in Sun Valley. I'll be thinking of you."

He kissed me one last time as the sun was smiling down on us. It all felt so right.

21

Anticipation

Back in Los Angeles, I went home to my lonely castle on the hill. It wasn't really a castle, but it was way too big of a house for me now that I was alone. The two-story, four-bedroom, three-bath, ranch-style home on an acre of land was way more than I needed.

The next day, I went back to work on a television movie called *Tagget*, which starred Daniel J. Travanti. I arrived early in the morning on the set and greeted the stunt coordinator, my friend, Don Pike. As always, I carried my Red Bag of Courage, though I never really knew exactly what the stunt would be until I arrived on the set. I trusted Don to tell me if there was an extra complicated stunt that I needed to prepare for and bring extra gear. Many times, the director would change his mind and decide to do something different from what was written in the script. So, I always came prepared with elbow, knee, hip, tailbone, and forearm pads, shin guards, butt protector, boob shield, mouth guard, and whatever else I could think of to keep me safe.

I was told that I would be doing a fight scene with stuntman Gary Pike, Don's younger brother, with whom I'd worked in South Africa and, as a result, shared a special bond. The director walked the stunt coordinator, Gary, and I step-by-step around a huge living room that was overcrowded with eclectic furniture. There were torchiere lamps, coffee tables with bunches of glass collectibles, wingback chairs, end tables with vases holding birds of paradise, and one long flowered couch with a high back. The director wanted us to demolish everything in sight as we struggled and fought our way through the flying debris.

Walking our path over and over as ballet dancers would practice a routine, we verbally reviewed the planned attack.

"I kick you in the shin, you grab my hair, I knock you into the lamp, you break a vase over my back, I punch you in the stomach, you tackle me to the ground, I try to get up, you knock me into the coffee table with the flying figurines. Then I stumble to the couch, you jump on top of me and attempt to strangle me to death. I try to get away . . ." It was helpful to recite the routine in order to have it stick in our minds.

After rehearsing this action in slow speed numerous times so the cameramen could figure out the best angles for the shots, Gary and I were ready. Of course, by now, it was time for lunch, and we had to break. After all, this was television, and the budget could not afford meal penalties if we didn't break at the union's scheduled times per contract. I really didn't feel like eating, knowing that I had this enormous fight scene to do. So, I went and nibbled on a small salad and watched Gary chowing down heavily. I kept going over the choreography in my head and visualizing the fight going perfectly as planned.

As our lunch break ended, I returned to the set where the hairdresser adjusted my hideous wig and slammed a few more bobby pins into my scalp. Ready as ever, I looked over at Gary and gave him the thumbs-up. The director yelled, "Camera's rolling, and action!"

As all hell broke loose, the choreographed ballet was suddenly a fight for survival. Lamps smashing, Gary groaning as I hit him in the stomach, me screaming as he grabbed my arm and threw me against the wall. When I tackled him and bulldogged him into the coffee table, glass shattered. We knew that as long as we smashed everything in sight, per our orders, we could improvise along the way. Finally, he violently threw me on the couch, and I struggled to get away. He launched himself on top of me and toppled the couch over backward. When I landed hard on his stomach, he blew the biggest fart that I ever heard in my life! Everyone on the set started laughing, and the director was almost in tears from laughter when he yelled, "Cut!"

Gary scoffed, "Diane!" and tried to blame it on me, but everyone on set knew it was Gary with his sheepish grin. That was a print, and we were wrapped. The director said it was the best fight he ever witnessed, and the best laugh he had had in a long, long time.

After saying my goodbyes, I headed home. On the doorstep was a package from Texas. Running inside, I tore open the brown paper to find three small boxes wrapped in colorful butterfly wrapping paper. I carefully opened the pretty paper and there was French perfume by Boucheron in a stunning blue bottle. It smelled delicious—like a breath of springtime air in Paris. Opening the other boxes, I found powder and body lotion all in matching deep blue containers.

Jack had included a simple note that read, "Till Sun Valley, I'll be thinking of you, Jack."

I called him that evening to thank him, but he was frazzled and said he couldn't talk. I could hear women's voices in the background. Jack had told me that he was divorced, but the truth was that I didn't really know much about his private life. I was extremely disappointed and thought, *He's a liar just like all the rest of them.*

The phone rang early the next morning as I was putting on my red cowboy boots and tan Stetson. I was preparing to exercise a Peruvian Paso horse named Stormy owned by Fred, an older neighbor in Simi Valley. Fred was a jolly, round-faced, eighty-something-year-old, loveable fat guy with eyebrows that looked like small hedges that needed trimming. Fred had a bad leg that was always wrapped up, and he limped like Quasimodo to the stable that was behind his house. He loved Stormy but was in no shape to ride the mighty steed. Crown Royal whiskey was Fred's closest friend, and it had taken cruel revenge on his body and mind.

Stormy was a strong black stallion with a long flowing mane, super wide back, and a charcoal tail with silver highlights that cascaded like a waterfall from his hindquarters. Peruvian Pasos were known to have the smoothest of gaits, sometimes referred to as the Cadillac of rides. Throwing their front legs sideways, their rumps glided along so the rider had a flying carpet sensation. I enjoyed riding Stormy for hours on the winding trails in the hills behind my home.

As I adjusted my Stetson in the mirror, Jack explained that he was sorry that he hadn't been able to talk the night before. I let him know that I was concerned that he was newly divorced and still in that twilight stage before being ready for a relationship. I told him that I wasn't sure if I wanted to meet him in Sun Valley, and that I would have to give it some more thought. He surprised me by saying that he understood and if I decided not to meet him in Sun Valley, he would still always cherish the time we'd had together. He didn't try to convince me to go on the next rendezvous, and I liked that. Assuring him that I would let him know in the next couple of days, I went to ride in the wide-open spaces where I had plenty of time to weigh matters out in my head.

Stormy was always very frisky when I first hopped on his back, trying to see what he could get away with, tossing his giant head and thick neck and rearing up like the wild stallion that he was. He would feel my legs tighten around his girth and hear my voice telling him to "Settle down, big boy," and we'd trot off down the bridle path to the entrance of the mountain park. Though the sun was shining brightly, as usual, there was a canopy of cool shade from the mighty oak trees. The mountain path was steep and rocky, but Stormy was sure-footed and, huffing and puffing, navigated the trail. I didn't mind the work he was putting in because, like his owner, Stormy could stand to lose a few pounds.

As we explored, I thought about Jack and the exciting, romantic time we'd shared in Aspen. Was it worth opening my heart to a guy who lived so far away? I was not really dating anyone special, and no one I had dated before had ever treated me to a first date like Jack had.

Stormy and I stopped by a picnic table where there was a trough of water. Dismounting, I loosened his girth and let him have a long drink of cool water.

Petting his wet nose and looking into his liquid brown eyes I queried, "Stormy, what do you think, boy? Should I go meet Jack in Sun Valley?"

He nodded his head up and down, but perhaps he was only trying to get the fly out of his ear! I laughed to myself, having the answer that I knew deep in my heart I wanted. Tightening his girth, we headed down the hill. Stormy loved to run fast back to the barn, and I let him have his fun.

When I got to the barn, Fred was nowhere in sight. I unsaddled Stormy, washed him off with the hose, and walked him around until he was dry. Leading him into his stall, I fed him a few carrots and kissed his velvet muzzle.

"See you next time buddy," I cooed.

Knocking on Fred's back door, I called to say goodbye. He asked me if I would like to have a "short one." That meant Crown Royal on the rocks.

"OK," I agreed reluctantly. "Just make it very short for me and add lots of water, please."

It tasted horrible, but I felt sorry for Fred and wanted to give him some company. Just as he usually did, Fred hobbled back with a short one for me and a huge, tall one for him. We clinked glasses and I told him about the beautiful ride that Stormy and I had had. Then Fred started crying and told me how much he missed his wife who had passed away two years earlier. I always tried to tell him positive things like "remember the good times, Fred" and "she wouldn't want you to be sad," but mostly I would just listen and feel his pain while slowly sipping the horrible-tasting whiskey.

Later that day, I made the stupid mistake of going to my tae kwon do class after having had the "short one." After putting on my gi and tightening my belt, I brushed my teeth and headed out to see Master Kim. I was in a class with all kids who came after school. I knew that the more I trained, the more jobs would be available to me. Plus, it was a great workout, and I knew that following my dream meant staying in tip-top shape.

Master Kim looked at me, squinting his eyes. He barked orders at us, and we performed choreographed routines, kicking and punching. But my timing was really off, late with kicks and I missed two punches.

Master Kim screamed inches away from my bright-red face, "Try harder, try harder!"

Then we began to spar. One short, chubby kid kicked me in the side of the knee, and I went down hard. I barely finished the class. I couldn't quit, but I was totally exhausted. After sparring, we all sat on the floor, legs crossed, to breathe and cool down.

Looking frustrated, Master Kim growled, "Someone do something before class, no good. Next time stay home."

I knew he was talking to me. I never went to class again after having consumed a "short one."

When I returned home, I elevated my leg and put an ice pack on it. I'd still been considering whether I should go to Sun Valley and meet Jack one more time to see if there was the possibility of a real relationship there. The long distance was definitely a negative factor, and his recent divorce was another. Recalling the sweet and hot connection we had in Aspen, I decided that one more encounter would give me the answers I was looking for.

When I called Jack to deliver the good and bad news, he was thrilled to hear my voice and said he was hoping that I would call. I told him I really wanted to get to know him better and that I would meet him in Sun Valley. He was elated. But I also told him that I got kicked in the knee in class and wasn't sure if I could ski or not. Jack assured me that it didn't matter if I was able to ski, and that just being together would make him the happiest guy on the planet. That sounded wonderful to me, and I looked forward to our next rendezvous.

The next day when I went to see my orthopedic doctor Dr. Rosenfeld in Beverly Hills, he waved his Super Bowl ring in my face reminding me, "You can have this if you'll marry me." He loved to flirt, in a sweet, harmless way. After X-raying my knee, he said I had a partially torn posterior cruciate ligament. As he lectured me on not doing things where I could get hurt, it seemed as though he forgot for a moment that I was a stuntwoman! I pleaded with him to give me some sort of knee brace so I could go skiing the next week.

He just shook his head and said, "Okay, but be careful. And no more tae kwon do for you. Next kick to that knee and you'll be in surgery!"

His assistant brought in a horrible-looking black contraption that fit like a tourniquet around my knee, sporting metal hinges on the sides to support my injured knee. I wasn't thrilled about it, but I was determined to ski in Sun Valley and see if Jack and I had a future together.

Deciding to be proactive, I bought my own ticket to Sun Valley. I didn't want to feel obligated to stay there if I discovered something weird or unpleasant about Jack or the situation. He began calling me every night to chat, and I was feeling like I was getting to know him a little better. During one phone conversation, Jack asked me what my favorite beverage was, and I said, "Champagne, Dom Pérignon to be exact." I loved the taste of fine bubbly and I loved that he cared.

However, during our conversations, another red flag popped up: this was his second divorce, and he lived with her for nine years but was only married a year.

What in the world could happen after all that time? I thought to myself.

I wouldn't wait nine years for any guy to marry me. Jack told me that she began cheating on him and that's why they split up.

In my mind, that seemed like a good enough reason for him to leave her.

None of the red flags I was noticing were enough to keep me from eagerly anticipating our rendezvous at Sun Valley.

Meanwhile, I was nursing my knee back to health by taking it slow around the house, which wasn't easy for me. I was usually juggling a myriad of activities: horseback riding, dirt bike riding, tae kwon do, and the gym, along with softball practice! So, slowing down meant grinding all my activities to a screeching halt.

I got a call from Conrad Palmisano, the stunt coordinator and friend with whom I worked so many times before.

"Hey Diane, can you fly to New York tomorrow?" he queried. "I'm doing a movie with Steven Segal and there's a little part in it for you and a cool car chase, too."

I worried about my knee and also being back in time to fly to Sun Valley. It never fails—if you plan a vacation, you always get called for work. I knew the car chase would be no problem for my knee, but the acting gave me pause. Would it involve running or jumping or being tackled or blown up?

I really didn't want to seem overly concerned so I just said laughingly, "Am I going to be another hooker that gets beat up, or what?"

Connie said, "No, you're a mom and you just get your head blown off!"

That I could do.

Connie assured me I'd be back in Los Angeles two days before I was scheduled to leave for Sun Valley. I really didn't like to call it that close, but I wanted to work, and I definitely wanted to see Jack again. Besides, the work would keep me occupied and not thinking about the future. Plus, I would get to see my mom and dad, too.

"Okay," I agreed, "I'm in. See you in New York City."

I flew to New York the next day with my well-worn leather Red Bag of Courage. The movie was called *Out for Justice*. I arrived on the set early the following morning and noticed that I would be driving an old, dumpy, beat-up station wagon. I took the car for a spin around the block to make sure the brakes, especially the emergency brake, were working properly. I also liked to get a feel for the "play" in the wheel of the car and check the tire air pressure. All these crucial items make or break the ability to handle the car once the action begins.

I went to hair and makeup, and they gave me a frumpy-looking hairdo with a teased bouffant top and a bit of a flip on the bottom. My makeup was plain Jane with light pink lipstick. I resembled a simple burbs housewife on the way to pick up the kids in the beat-up station wagon.

On action, I whipped around a busy corner in Brooklyn. A Camaro with three guys smoking crack inside was blocking my path.

Blowing the horn impatiently, I rolled down the window and screamed, "Move the goddamn car!"

I leaned on the horn again and again.

The passenger with watery bloodshot eyes shouted, "Are you talking to me?"

I yelled, "Yeah, move the goddamn car!"

With that, Bad Billy stormed over to my car in a rage and yanked me up by the hair, pulled me halfway out of the car and shot me in the head! I was wired with a blood bag that was attached to a small explosive charge, and when the shot went off, the blood bag was exploded by the special effects guy detonating the explosive charge. But the charge was too big! It sent blood flying across the street almost hitting a crowd of locals gathered on the busy corner. Everyone screamed in horror. I just lay there hanging upside down, dangling over the car door until I heard the director yell cut.

"Let's do another take and easy on the blood!" explained the director.

I had to have the blood washed out of my hair, dried, then reset, as well as being given a clean fresh wardrobe. And after a lengthy pause, we were ready to go again. Bad Billy grabbed me and shot me again, and this time the blood amount was under control, and it was a print! The crowd went crazy clapping and hollering.

We moved on to do some car chases around the piers in Brooklyn. The dance of the car chase always excited me to no end. Connie choreographed each move like a master. He played out the sequence with toy cars on the pavement so we would know exactly where to drive and what to do with our vehicles. It was a full day of sliding around corners and plenty of near misses galore. As the sun set, we said our goodbyes and exchanged our bear hugs. I drove to New Jersey to visit my parents and was back on the plane home to LA the next morning.

The day finally arrived when I was leaving for Sun Valley. Determined to ski, if only on the intermediate slopes, I made sure I packed my unattractive but necessary knee brace. I even bought a new black ski outfit with a form-fitting top and wide leg pants that could hide my knee brace. Jack was flying in with two buddies, the dentists who I met in Aspen, and my plane was due in a few hours before his. He said that I should go directly to the hotel, which was at the base of the mountain close to the ski lifts. The keys would be waiting for me at the front desk. After checking in, I grabbed the keys and ran up to the room. It was an enormous suite with a chandelier in the living room and a cozy fireplace. There was a huge bouquet of exotic flowers sitting on the coffee table with a note that I immediately tore open.

"Can't wait to be with you, Jack."

Next to the flowers was an ice bucket with a bottle of Dom chilling with two champagne glasses.

Very nice touch, I thought.

I strolled out onto the balcony and let the warm sun caress my face as I breathed in the fresh mountain air. I wondered if this trip would live up to my expectations or if I would head home in a hurry.

After a while, Jack called to say that his plane was delayed. I began to notice that the anticipation was making me restless and nervous. I walked around the little village, did some window shopping, and tried to eat a tiny Caesar salad in a quaint Tyrolean restaurant. I rehearsed in my head what I would say to Jack and wondered how I would feel seeing him again. I wandered back to the room and snuggled into the red overstuffed down sofa. The television was on, but I couldn't concentrate on anything. My head was filled with dreams of love and passion, and only time would tell if, this time, this man would be the one.

When I heard a knock on the door and the key opening, I bolted up on the couch.

Jack rushed in saying, "Hi honey, I'm home."

I ran to meet him, and he gave me the biggest hug ever and twirled me around in his arms. He looked surprisingly better than the last time I saw him. He was sporting a great tan and smiling with those perfect teeth. It appeared that he had lost a few pounds and firmed up the body, too! His shirt was open just enough to reveal a blanket of inviting fur on his chest.

Spotting the champagne he said, "I ordered that for you."

I smiled and said, "I saved it for us."

He popped the cork and we toasted to a week of great skiing in Sun Valley. We made small talk about his plane delays and what I did to fill the waiting hours. Then he took his finger and gently outlined my lips. He wrapped me in his arms and kissed me deeply. His mustache felt soft and smelled like fresh breath mints. I liquefied in his arms and remembered our romantic night in Aspen. Now I had him all to myself for a whole week.

Together we strolled out to the balcony and gazed at the sparkling stars in the clear sky above the chair lift. A light snow began falling and we would have fresh powder to play on in the morning. Jack asked how my knee was holding up.

I answered, "I'm skiing, no matter what! My knee brace will hold it together for me, but I need to take it easy."

He said, "We can take lots of breaks and just enjoy the day and being with each other."

I liked that. We headed inside to the huge, inviting, king-size bed with the giant soft down comforter. We fell into each other's arms and the night turned into day much too soon.

Early the next morning, we strolled hand in hand into the breakfast room. Smells of hot cooking bacon and fresh coffee wafted all around us. His friends were gathered at a huge table staring at us and looking for signs of satisfaction on his face or mine.

Bob laughed and said, "So, Jack, how was your night?"

I just smiled and watched Jack puff out his chest and wink at his friends. I really didn't want to ski with all of them. Not only did I have to take it easy with my knee, but I also wanted to be alone with my man. After enjoying a hearty breakfast, Jack told the other guys we would meet them for lunch on the mountain. He carried my skis, and off we trudged to the lift, which was very close by. My knee brace felt like a monstrosity wrapped around my leg. I didn't want to complain and spoil the mood of this brand-new day we were about to share. Hopping on the lift, we cuddled all the way to the top of the mountain feeling a real magical connection. Though I'd usually be racing down the diamond or double black diamond runs, I suggested we start on an intermediate slope. At one point, we were skiing too close together and our skis crossed, and I went down hard on my knee. I screamed in pain and Jack was right there expressing concern and taking the blame for my fall. He was so compassionate, which I appreciated a lot.

I made a mental note that he seemed different from most of the uncaring jerks whom I'd been dating. He helped me up and we slowly skied back to the lodge to take a break. We found an enormous soft sofa directly in front of a roaring fire in a massive stone fireplace. Sipping on yummy hot cider drinks that warmed our tummies, we laughed a lot and talked about our experiences growing up on the East Coast. We discussed our families, and he seemed remarkably close to his parents and his two sisters. After we finished our drinks, Jack asked me if I'd like to go shopping. He wanted to buy me a souvenir of Sun Valley, something for me to remember him by. I was glad to take a break from skiing and I loved shopping, so we went from store to store looking for an unusual item.

Suddenly, I spotted a painting of an Indian Spiritual Warrior, beautifully framed. He looked like he was floating in the clouds with the sun and the moon and eagle feathers in his hair. His face looked wise and serene, and I felt he was meant to be mine. Perhaps to put blessings on our new love. When I said that I would love to have him for my house, Jack picked up the painting and carried it to the cash register. He told the clerk to wrap it up carefully for the plane flight to Los Angeles. The Spiritual Warrior was going to be one of my guardian angels.

22

Crazy in Love and Juggling My Career

After our time together in Sun Valley, thoughts of a future with Jack began to fill my mind.

A lot of those thoughts happened while floating in my pool. When I was working, my concentration and focus was so intense that when I was between jobs, I gravitated to peaceful, easygoing lifestyle. Relaxing in an oversized float big enough for two with a pillow top and drink holders, I could smell the sweet aroma of the horses nearby and listen to the birds chirping in the trees. Floating in a blissful state, noticing the puffy cloud formations, I imagined my possible future with Jack. I was writing the script of Jack and Diane in my head where I could control everything, including the happy ending. How I longed for that to come true. Since our trip to Sun Valley, we had a number of rendezvous, all very much like mini honeymoons where the break in our togetherness made our reunions like Fourth of July celebrations. We visited Mexico, Jackson Hole, Deer Valley, and Taos to name a few. Each was wonderful as I got to know him better, but he never invited me to his home in Texas. I was beginning to wonder why. Texas wasn't the ideal vacation spot, but I wanted to see where and how he managed his everyday life.

When I invited Jack to my house in California for a sun-kissed vacation, he said he would love to visit my home. He knew I loved to golf, so he also planned a getaway to La Quinta in Palm Springs for a few days. *That was the plan.* Lo and behold, the vacation/work theory kicked in as usual. No sooner had we planned our vacation than the phone began to ring with new work.

The call was for a job that would take place the second night of Jack's visit. I was beginning to let our relationship interfere with my work, which I never did before. Consistently out of town or unavailable, I was losing focus on the dream and channeling that energy into being with Jack.

I was president of the Stuntwomen's Association of Motion Pictures, and the ladies were complaining that I was not around to run most of the monthly meetings anymore. I'd been the president for seven years and felt it was time someone else took over the time-consuming job anyway.

When my answering service called me regarding my availability for the job, I told them I would call them back in ten minutes. I wanted to call Jack to hear his reaction before I accepted the work. Describing the offer to work on the movie *Die Trying* with Don the Dragon Wilson, I explained that it was a night shot, which meant that I could be in and out of there in an hour or, possibly, I could work till daybreak. Jack had booked a room that night for a private casita at La Quinta along with a golf reservation for the next morning.

Without hesitation, Jack encouraged, "Take the job and I'll go with you. I've never been on a movie set before."

Because it was an unwritten rule that you never brought outsiders with you to work, I had never taken any guests to the set with me before, except my dad and mom in New York City. But for Jack, I was willing to break all the rules.

Booked to do a car chase, I arrived on the set located in downtown Los Angeles around five o'clock and greeted the stunt coordinator, Patrick Statham. Pat was a younger, enthusiastic stuntman who was once in a seminar of mine and Vince Deadrick Jr.'s at UCLA on the business of doing stunts. I am sure I made a point of saying, "Do not bring friends with you to work." And this was the first time that I was working for Pat. Introducing Jack to Pat, I explained that we were leaving for Palm Springs directly after the wrap. It was true, but a flimsy excuse for bringing him with me to work. Jack was dressed in expensive black silk blended slacks and a colorful Gucci silk shirt with shiny black Salvador Ferragamo shoes. I instructed him to keep a low profile while I was getting ready and rehearsing the shot. Several crew members asked me if he was the producer. After all, he had the money bag strut.

Focusing my mind on the job I had to do, I walked the route of the car chase several times with the stunt coordinator and the other drivers. I had to slide around a number of corners, do a few near misses with oncoming cars, dart into an alley where a waiter carrying a gigantic platter of linguini almost steps into my path, then slide around a final corner and slam into a dumpster. I was driving a hot black Camaro and being chased by guys in a sleek red Firebird. After walking the route a half-dozen times with the drivers in the oncoming cars, I went to hair and makeup to get ready. They plopped a stupid-looking wig on me, once again, and some bright-red lipstick. I went back to my trailer to slip into my very, very low-cut blouse. Like someone would notice my low-cut blouse in the middle of a ripping car chase! At least when you are at the wheel, you do not have to put the skirt or pants on from wardrobe. You wear your own. You also have the luxury of wearing your own driving shoes and not some ridiculous high heels. At the time, short black Reeboks were the preferred stunt shoe.

Meanwhile, Jack was hanging out in my trailer. When I walked in, he laughed so hard, grabbed me, and we started making out big time! When it was time to emerge, I fixed my lipstick and was ready to go. When they called for a lunch break at midnight, I could see it was going to be an all-night affair. After introducing Jack to a few stunt guys, I nibbled on a salad. I could never eat much before a stunt, no matter what the stunt was.

When lunch was over, I hopped back into my Camaro, ready to roll. Don the Dragon decided that he wanted to ride passenger instead of having the stuntman double him. It's always awkward to have the lead actor riding along because I must tell them to hang on and shut up! Also, if there's a screw up, like crashing and hurting the lead actor, a driver is in deep trouble. If the lead actor gets hurt and can't continue, the show is forced to wrap until the actor is better, which costs the production company hundreds of thousands of dollars. The insurance companies have policies against this happening as well, but many times the actors insist on doing their own stunts and it's a delicate situation.

So, when Don the Dragon jumped in the car next to me, I calmly explained what the action was to be and told him I needed him to buckle up his seat belt, be quiet, and enjoy the ride. Thankfully, he was cool with that. I got a nod and a deep breath from him and "Action" from the director. Putting the pedal to the metal, I burned rubber taking off. The camera loves those smoking tires. Sliding around the first turn and fishtailing back, I hopped over the curb and cut the wheel sharply back and forth, racing down the narrow street as an oncoming car was coming straight at us. As rehearsed, I held my position as the other car dove onto the sidewalk, nearly hitting us head-on. I then slid into the dark alley and the waiter stepped out of the back door of a restaurant with the platter of linguini. I almost hit him, as planned, and when he threw the linguini platter in the air it crashed onto my windshield. I couldn't see a thing! The thick crème sauce was like an opaque veil of goo.

Because Don's side of the windshield was basically clearer than mine, I yelled, "Tell me when to turn! Tell me when to turn!"

Flipping on my windshield wipers I strained to see through the goo.

"Turn now!" shouted Don the Dragon.

Sliding around the final turn, I slammed the brakes on, and plowed into the dumpster.

The Dragon let out a yell, "EEEEEYA!"

We were both safe. My heart was beating like drum, but I was visibly cool. I hi-fived Don and hopped out of the car. It was day-break and it was time to wrap! I said my goodbyes and jumped into my Corvette with Jack who kept saying how amazing I was and how much he enjoyed watching me work. We drove to Palm Springs, golfed eighteen holes, went out to dinner, and made love all night!

23

Deliberate Blindness

The headline read, "Chuck Norris to Do New Television Show in Dallas."

Skimming the paper, I almost choked on my cappuccino. I was reclining in my favorite lounge chair while reading the *Hollywood Reporter* on a spectacular sunny day in Simi Valley. Grabbing the phone, I called Eric Norris, Chuck's son, who was a stuntman and stunt coordinator. I'd worked with Eric, who had an incredible smile and a winning personality, on several jobs over the years. We always hit it off.

"Hey, Eric," I said, "I just read that your dad is doing a show in Dallas. I'm dating a guy that lives in Plano, Texas and I'd really like to work on the show."

"Sure, Diane," he agreed, "I think you would make a great double for the female lead, Sheree Wilson. I'll figure out the shooting schedule and fly you in to meet her."

"That's great!" I said, "Can't wait to see you and meet Sheree. Thanks a million."

When I called Jack to tell him the good news he said, "I guess it was meant to be."

The dream of having steady stunt work on a television show was looking promising, plus having this guy who I really cared about nearby was nothing short of a miracle. Eric called back the next day and said he had a part for me to play on the first episode.

"Don't get your hopes up for a recurring role," he explained. "You're playing a reporter and interviewing a guy in a car, and the car and you get blown up! I talked to Sheree and she's excited to meet you as well."

"Sounds perfect," I chimed. "Thank you so much, see you in Dallas."

On the hot scorching day when I few into Dallas, most of the grass was brown and the earth was parched from the blistering sun and lack of rain. My previous vision of Texas was cowboy hats and cattle herds, and neither one was in sight!

Jack picked me up in his old, beat-up Cadillac Eldorado. Because I drove a shiny new Corvette and loved beautiful cars, I thought it was weird for a dentist to own that kind of car. But I was thrilled to be with him in Texas. I laughed playfully about his car, and he explained that he really didn't care about cars. That was obvious! It was so wonderful to see him again and we kissed madly on the curb until the airport police chased us down the road. I was saving the production company money by having Jack pick me up and staying at his house rather than them putting me up at a nearby hotel.

Jack had a modest brick house in a boring neighborhood where all the houses looked alike. It had a small backyard with no pool and a six-foot tattered fence shielding the backyard from the alley. The interior of the house appeared to be decorator-done in shades of gray with a black lacquer master bedroom suite. It wasn't about the house, furniture, or crappy cars; it was Jack with whom I longed to be.

The house smelled like cigarette smoke, which he tried to cover up with air freshener and burning candles. I told him if he smoked cigarettes, he didn't need to sneak them. Looking at me sheepishly, he confessed. I also found empty vodka bottles hidden in the closet and under the bathroom sink. I chose to ignore some obvious warning signs and allowed myself to be wrapped up in the soft cashmere blanket of his love.

When I arrived on the set the next day, it was blazing hot. I was about to meet Sheree and I was sweating like a piglet in a roasting pit. Our hair color was nearly a match, and so the hairdresser on the set just pinned my hair under to simulate Sheree's shorter style. If the hairdresser can get away without using a wig, it looks much better on camera. Wigs tend to look fake, especially if they are inexpensive ones. I noticed from afar that Sheree appeared to be a bit taller than I am, so I put my high-heeled boots on and mopped my brow with the wads of tissue with which the makeup lady armed me. I was wearing long, tight-fitting brown jeans and an imitation suede shirt that was soaking wet. As the reporter in the scene, this was to be my wardrobe.

I thought to myself, *Why can't they pick something cooler to wear?* But I just went with the flow and tried to deal with it. I didn't want to make waves, and I really wanted Sheree to like me and approve me to be her stunt double.

As I tucked in a loose bobby pin, Eric came around the corner and grabbed my arm and said, "Let's go meet my dad and Sheree."

He introduced me to Chuck who was smiling and super warm and friendly.

Chuck said, "*Diane* . . . I won't forget your name, that was my ex-wife's name."

We all laughed, and I felt welcomed. Chuck looked even better in person than he did on screen. He had smiling eyes, a beautiful grin, and was in fantastic shape.

"Glad to have you with us," he beamed.

Sheree sauntered over and shook my hand as Eric introduced us. She had high cheekbones and piercing blue eyes. She was outgoing and eager to hear about my experience. I told her I was an excellent all-around stuntwoman and that I would love to double her on the show for all her stunts.

I explained earnestly, "Car chases, horses, motorcycles, explosions, fights: I can do it all."

She eyed me up and down and said, "Great, you're in."

I gave her a big hug and off she went. Wow! I was in! Doubling the lead in a television show meant steady work, residuals, and—in this case—time to spend in Texas with my lover, Jack. My dream was coming true once again. I was thrilled.

Eric and I hopped in a van and were transported to the courthouse steps in Dallas. In the scene, I had a clipboard in hand, and I was trying to take notes and run down the stairs with a pack of reporters all screaming questions at the bad guy who had just been acquitted. I pushed my way to the front of the pack and through the police barricade as the bad guy jumped into his car.

I ran up to the window yelling, "How does it feel to be free? How does it feel to be free?"

Then suddenly, the car exploded and burst into flames.

The concussion knocked me down onto the blistering tarmac. I was supposed to be dead, so I couldn't move an inch as the skin on my arm began to scald.

Oh God, please call cut *now!* raced through my head.

There was a camera tight on me, so I didn't dare to budge.

Finally, the director yelled, "Cut!"

Yeow! My arm was burned and beginning to blister. The medic ran in and sprayed some cooling gel on it. That's when I realized that I should not have rolled my sleeves up. Live and learn. I acted like it was no big deal, but it hurt like hell. Thank God I had long pants on, or my legs would have been scorched, too! I was praying that we didn't have to do a second take.

"Great shot, we're moving on," the director announced.

What a relief.

That night when I got home to Jack's house with my arm bandaged, he was very sweet and kind. It felt good to have someone to care about me and pamper me. After ordering Chinese food, he gave me a fabulous foot rub. Those foot rubs melted my heart.

I told Jack I didn't really like Texas. It was too darn hot, and everything looked dead. I could see in his eyes that he was hurt because he really wanted me to like it.

He said, "If you move here, we could go on lots of vacations to the Caribbean to escape the heat."

I just laughed and said, "I'm not moving anywhere till I get married."

Grateful to have the job on a series, and to be able to see my boyfriend regularly, I began flying back and forth from Los Angeles to Dallas on a regular basis. One day at home in Simi Valley, I was staring at the book that Jack gave me about love stories of famous couples. A photo of Tracy and Hepburn looking very much in love adorned the book's jacket. The story of their forbidden love was that he was married to another woman while cavorting around with Katherine. Flipping the pages, I saw Bogart and Bacall frolicking in the grass. He was many years her senior. I couldn't help but wonder what our unfolding love story would bring. I read and reread what Jack had written on the first page. *He never met anyone like me, and he would be counting the days until we were together again. He was filled with warm memories and cherished the time that we spent together.*

How could I know if this relationship would develop into the kind of love stories found inside the pages of this book? There were a few red flags, but I rationalized that that was always the case. No one is perfect, and I was hoping that some fatal flaw would not raise its ugly head any time soon. Having dated a guy from New Jersey for almost a year before the relationship fizzled out due to the distance, I also knew that long-distance relationships were difficult. Ah, but this was *Texas,* a lot closer than New Jersey. I told myself that to make it seem all right. He was Jewish, I am Catholic. But there is only one God, I reassured myself. He was divorced twice. I was divorced once. So, I concluded, we picked the wrong partners.

But the biggest red flag of all was that he had a fourteen-year-old daughter whom he had not seen in several years. Enjoying such a special relationship with my father, I couldn't fathom that. Jack seemed very bitter about the situation and blamed it all on his ex-wife, saying that she had poisoned the kid against him and that all he ever did was send the child money for support, which he clearly resented. Although I wondered what the real story was behind the wall of silence between a daughter and her father, I wanted to paint the rosy picture and erase the dark clouds in my mind. I was allowing myself to have another dream of having a loving relationship for the rest of my life.

Still browsing through the book, my pager went off and it snapped me back to reality. I called Teddy's, and they told me a stunt coordinator for whom I had never worked before was trying to reach me for a job. They gave me his number and I quickly called him back.

"Diane, I have this 150-foot descender job to do on Friday and you would be the perfect double for the actress." He asked, "Do you still weigh 120 pounds?"

I wanted to say, "Sorry, I ballooned up to 150 pounds," and eliminate the agony of the anticipation of the high drop, but I cheerfully said, "Yes, I hopped on the scale this morning—120 on the nose."

Overcoming my fear of heights was always a challenge, something that took all of my inner strength to accomplish. It required every ounce of courage inside me not only to overcome my fear of heights, but to also look cool to the stunt coordinator and the rest of the crew when I had the daunting task of doing high falls. I was willing to put my entire being to the test because I knew that I could overcome my fear.

"Okay then," he said. "I'll call you tomorrow and let you know the time for Friday morning."

I hung up the phone and wondered why I had said yes. But I knew. It was the challenge, the test of my inner self. The fear began to bubble in my stomach as I prepped for Friday. I had never done a descender. The descender is a spool that attaches a cable to a harness that is secured on your body. As you leap off the building in a free fall, the cable unwinds and you hope that it stops you a few feet before you splat on the pavement.

Thoughts like *this will be my last ride* danced in my head as I quickly replaced them with images of a soft, featherbed landing for me.

I remembered that Six Flags Magic Mountain in Valencia had a free fall ride. I quickly phoned them and found out that they opened at ten o'clock the next morning. I could hardly sleep that night as dreams of falling and falling off skyscrapers rocketed through my brain. I would wake up sweating profusely just before I hit the ground only to fall asleep again and revisit the plunge through space.

Long before sunrise, I finally decided just to get up, just have a glass of water since I was afraid to eat anything, and head for my day at Magic Mountain. Like an eager child, I was the first one in line waiting for the ticket window to open. After buying my ticket, I ran directly to Freefall.

The tall, skinny, pimple-faced kid who was running the ride looked so young that I wondered if he knew how to operate the controls that would prevent the small gondola from crashing into the ground below. After nervously hopping in the car, I waited for the other positions to be filled. When a family of four piled in the cart and waited along side of me, I actually felt calmer because there were others experiencing the drop from the sky with me. The door locked shut and my heart raced as the cart was gently pulled to the top of the tower some one hundred feet above the earth. I noticed the freckle-faced, red-headed kid across from me who was jumping up and down, not cringing in fear like I was. My hands began to grip the posts tighter as we slowly reached the top.

After a brief pause, the cart suddenly dropped, and we plunged at lightning speed to the tarmac below. At the last second, the cart eased to a stop, just as I hoped my descender would the following day.

My mouth was dry as I exited the ride and sighed a deep breath.

Now I can do this job on Friday, I thought to myself.

Hopping back in line, I waited to ride the vertical drop once again and continued the exercise in courage all day long.

The wise-ass kid operating the ride said, “Hey lady, don’t you want to try the roller coaster?”

“No thanks,” I smiled.

I was determined to master the free fall without getting butterflies in my stomach. By the end of the day, the fall was as easy to me as falling out of a hammock! Confident and ready, I was mentally prepared for my big job. Bring it on!

Some people assume that stuntpeople are crazy, fearless, or both. While I suppose an argument could be made for the first, I can say with certainty that we are not immune to fear. We have a lot of the same fears as everyone else. The human body actually produces a fear response to protect us. And for that reason, it’s worth noticing. The problem comes when we allow ourselves to be *bullied* by our fears. When we miss out on social events because they make us feel anxious. Or when we fail to apply for the promotion because we’re afraid we won’t get it. Or when we avoid taking the healthy risk that might get us where we want to be. Fear stops being a healthy protector when it bullies and controls us.

I can’t tell you how fantastic it felt to conquer my fear of the free fall descender. I felt invincible! If there’s a fear that’s holding you back, I encourage you to tackle it today. Face it. Don't let it be the boss of you. That might mean taking one big leap, like taking flying lessons to overcome your fear of flying. Or it might be a series of baby steps that help you to conquer whatever has been holding you back. When you avoid your fear, it wins. When you face it, you can accomplish anything. Tackle your fear and be proud of it.

Happily skipping to my car, I heard my pager start beeping. When I called my answering service, they said the stunt coordinator had called and my job was canceled!

I was really disappointed because I was totally ready for the plunge. However, deep inside I was relieved to not have to visit the doorway of fear in the morning. I headed home tired and weary, both mentally and physically, from the day of squishing the fear monster that lurked in my head. The monster lay dormant for the moment, but I knew he would be doing pushups in my head soon.

When I scanned the script for my next episode on *Walker*, I saw two of my favorite words: 18-wheeler. It wasn't the part that had been assigned to me, but I knew it was my sweet spot. So, the morning we began filming, I let Eric know I thought the stunt had my name on it.

"Hey, Eric," I said with a sweet smile, "I read the script and saw what's coming. Can I drive the 18-wheeler? I have my Class 1 license, and I'd *really* love to drive the truck."

"Oh," he informed me, "the guy who's bringing the truck is going to drive it."

I was disappointed but I understood.

A few days later when the truck scene was scheduled to be shot,

I was eating lunch with the guys, talking and laughing as we enjoyed the caterer's delicious meal.

When Eric got up to leave the table, he tossed me the keys to the 18-wheeler and said, "Diane, here ya go."

"Really?" I asked, wide-eyed.

He smiled and nodded yes.

I ran to the truck, hopped in, and adjusted my seat and mirrors.

Tony, the truck driver said, "Heard you were driving the truck. Can I ride passenger?"

I told him I would ask Eric. I didn't really want a passenger, but I was grateful that I was the one driving. And I knew the trucker would get the thrill of his life in the scene with the bus careening straight at us. Eric said it was okay, so I told Tony he could come along if he promised not to say a word.

We did several slow speed rehearsals with me driving the truck up a steep hill and approaching a sharp corner. The bus appeared and was speeding directly toward us. I was directed to hold my course, and Gary, the bus driver, would swerve at the last minute and miss hitting us. I trusted Gary and knew he was a great driver, but I could see Tony sweating and gripping the seat with white knuckles.

When Eric asked if we were ready, Gary and I said yes on our radios.

Asking Tony to hold the radio, I reminded him that silence was golden. I knew I needed to stay focused. On action, I dropped the truck into gear and began to lumber up the steep hill, then started to gain some speed as the bus came flying into view around the corner. Trusting the plan, I kept my speed and didn't hesitate for a second. The bus came straight at us and at the very last second swerved and missed us.

It was perfect! Tony was as white as a ghost and looked like he was in a state of shock. The director loved it but wanted to do one more with a different camera angle. When I asked Tony if he was okay and if he wanted to go again, he said it was the best thrill of his life. The second take was equally as exciting and maybe even a tad closer on the miss. After Gary hopped out of the bus, we gave each other bear hugs. Throughout the rest of the day, I kept thinking of my dad and all the days we spent truckin'! *Thank you, Dad.* His investment in me had paid off in so many ways.

Working on *Walker, Texas Ranger* was one of the most enjoyable experiences that I have had in television jobs. Chuck Norris was a joy to work with. He was always very personable and had a spirit of kindness and happiness that just flowed from him. His son, Eric, was amazing to work for too—easygoing and direct. Don Pike and his brother Gary, who were like brothers to me, were also involved in the show. So, the environment on the set was wonderful.

On another episode, I was driving the Walker truck and I was getting chased down the highway by a small two-seater plane. As I approached an overhead bridge, the plane was to gain altitude and fly over the bridge. On one take, the plane's wheels actually bounced off the roof of the truck that I was driving. It was a huge surprise for me to feel the plane hit the roof of the vehicle. Fortunately, the plane and the passengers were safe because that could have been a nasty crash.

In one of my favorite episodes, as a farmer's wife, I was playing Walker's mom when he was a little boy. While he was out plowing the field with his daddy, I came out of the cabin to ring the dinner bell and call them to supper. Just then, the bad guys came riding in and shot my husband in the field. They circled around me with their horses as I tried to run to help my son and husband. As my son approached, they backhanded him and began to drag me into the cabin. I fought and screamed as they pulled me into the pit of death. That moment as a boy, seeing what the bad guys did to his parents, is why Walker became a Texas Ranger. In addition to the stunts I loved, I really enjoyed playing parts like that one, describing myself as an "action actress."

On the action-packed show, I got to be involved in explosions, gunfights, car chases, horse work, and motorcycle work on many episodes. I still receive residuals today for all the wonderful work back then.

When you finally lock into your dream job, remember to be grateful. Always give 110 percent. Be on time and share your joy.

24

Dad's Eightieth

"Dad," I asked, "if you could go anywhere in the world, where would you go?"

We were golfing and my dad's eightieth birthday was approaching.

He didn't hesitate.

"Ah," he mused fondly, "it was always a dream of mine to go on the Orient Express." Without hesitation I assured him, "We're going"

"You're kidding!" he exclaimed.

I wasn't. My dad was everything to me and I wanted to thank him for helping me become the woman I was. He'd taught me to follow my dreams. He assured me that I could do anything I put my mind to. Whatever happened, he was always there for me. My father was by far the kindest, most loving, warm, and funniest human being I have ever met. He was always laughing and smiling, never complaining, and a joy to be around. He also looked great for his age: five feet, ten inches tall and toned with blondish, silver hair and turquoise eyes, his face lined from laughing all his life. His strong hands were like meat hooks from working hard doing the thing he loved—driving for his own company Plaza Trucking.

I immediately began researching and planning for our fabulous first-class train journey. When I read that there was a formal dining car, I asked my brother to get Dad a tuxedo for his birthday. Then, after booking the trip, I waited like a little kid for the day we'd take off.

Of course, I got called for a huge job after booking the trip, but nothing could stop me from spending that precious time with my dad. I would have loved for my mom to join us, but she was homebound with medical problems and unable travel.

We took off from JFK on the red-eye and arrived in Paris early the following morning. As the flight attendant fussed over us in the first-class cabin, I practiced *bonjour* and *merci* with my dad endlessly as we sipped champagne and toasted to our adventure. My dad had never been to Europe, and I was eager to show him around. I'd studied French in college, so I knew that I would understand a lot of the language when we got there.

The city was bustling with early-morning traffic as our taxi wove in and out around the other small European cars. I told the taxi driver in French where we were going, and my dad's eyes lit up.

He proudly responded with another phrase that I drilled into him, "Très bon!"

Everything was très bon, indeed. The Hôtel de Elysées was a charming little boutique hotel just off the Avenue des Champs-Élysées. I loved staying there because of the location and sweet ambience of the lobby café where we enjoyed strong coffee and fresh-baked croissants as the staff readied our chamber. The smell of those croissants made you melt, in a dreamlike state, into the plush burgundy velvet sofa.

"Bonjour," my dad proudly said to our pretty young waitress.

After our yummy croissants, the bellman escorted us up to our room in the world's tiniest elevator. We had to ride separately because only one person at a time would fit! Our room was decorated with Louis XIV-style furniture, ornate draperies, and twin beds with bedspreads that matched the drapes in flowering pastel colors. Beautiful fresh flowers awaited us in the room with a note card.

Tearing open the card, I read, "Bonjour mon amour, Jack."

I was impressed, as was my dad. He so wanted me to be happy.

When I asked my dad if he wanted to take a nap he said, "No, let's hit the town."

He was always energetic and raring to go even at eighty! We dropped our bags and headed to the Seine River to take the Bateau cruise where the guide explained, in several different languages, the significance of every low bridge we passed under. My dad was all eyes and ears, taking in the sights and sounds of the foreign land.

I was so grateful for the time we had together. The river cruise was a perfect way to spend a little time and get acquainted with the Paris ambience. After the cruise, we went to a tiny café on the Champs-Élysées and ordered some *petit dejeuner* and a bottle of French wine.

I talked to my dad about Jack and shared that there was a major issue with him: he didn't want to have a child. He'd had an unpleasant experience with his ex-wife after she took his daughter and moved away when she was only two years old. He said the reason he didn't have a relationship with her was because his ex made it exceedingly difficult for him to see her, which I found very sad and unimaginable—to have a child and not be in contact with them. I feared it might be my last chance to have the child I'd yearned to have for many years.

Playfully, my dad laughed and said, "Parenting isn't all it's cracked up to be!"

I couldn't ignore the possibility that I was too old already, and that at forty-two, I might have problems conceiving. I definitely was falling in love with Jack and needed to decide whether my future was to be with him but with no child. We actually had gone to see a therapist who he chose, a man, who summed up the issue by saying, "You can have any dog you want instead of a kid."

Somehow the "compromise" felt imbalanced.

I took my dad to the Folies Bergère, another dream of his, I discovered. Dad looked so elegant and handsome in his new tuxedo. I wore a short black velvet halter dress with killer high heels. I'm sure everyone thought I was his young babe. The topless dancing girls were gorgeous with extravagant costumes, and white-wigged waiters in uniforms marched down flights of stairs carrying the entrées on silver platters covered with shiny silver domes. When the four-man musical quartet came to our table, my dad asked them to play "My Diane," and shockingly, they knew it! Dad palmed a huge tip into the bass violinist's hand, and they played so beautifully as my dad beamed his broad unforgettable smile at me. Then he mimed playing the bass violin and I totally cracked up. We enjoyed the most beautiful evening together that I will never forget.

The next day, we decided we wanted to golf somewhere near Paris. So, we rented a car, got a map and directions, and drove about forty minutes outside of Paris where we miraculously found the golf course. Honestly, just getting around the Arc de Triomphe and out of the city was amazingly difficult. The driving was crazy, but of course I loved that. When we arrived at the golf course, I tried to explain to the pro shop attendant that we wanted a golf cart. When he seemed a bit confused, I thought it was because of my broken French. But then I realized that he was saying that they had only one golf cart and we needed to wait until it was returned. We opted for the pull carts and made our way onto the beautifully manicured fairways. We noticed they had lights set up for night golf, which was something we'd never seen before. Always laughing and joking, we hacked our way—or I should say I hacked *my* way—around the course. Dad, whose swing was smooth and effortless, was a great golfer and made it look easy. But I was always trying to "kill" the ball. After our game, we found a picturesque château and had a steak au poivre dinner that was off-the-charts fabulous.

The following morning, we arrived at the train station and were completely overwhelmed by the beauty of the elegant Orient Express train. A stylishly uniformed cabin concierge welcomed us aboard. As he escorted us to our stateroom, he explained that he was entirely at our service, day or night, for anything we might want or need. The gorgeous stateroom was finished in polished mahogany with crystal stemware and Irish linen towels. There was a bottle of Dom Pérignon chilling in a crystal ice bucket with a note.

It read, "Santé, mon amour."

Pretty impressive, I thought. Jack won some big points with that move!

Our young, handsome, efficient stateroom captain fluffed our down pillows and asked if he could bring us anything else, reminding us that he was available twenty-four hours a day for any need that we could possibly dream up.

Our journey from Paris would take us through Switzerland and Austria, finally stopping in Venice, Italy. I felt incredibly lucky for the three glorious nights on this enchanting, historic train with my beloved dad. Kings, queens, and movie stars had graced the corridors we were so blessed to be enjoying together.

Later that first evening, our captain escorted us to the formal dining car, my dad looking dashing in his new black tux and me in a black, sequined form-fitting cocktail dress adorned with ostrich feathers. The incredible, delicious seven-course dinner, paired with vintage French wines, was almost unfathomable. We feasted on Coquilles Saint-Jacques, Chateaubriand for two with béarnaise sauce to die for. Every morsel was a gastronomic delight. I arranged for a special, strawberry-filled birthday cake for my dad—which was his favorite—topped with nine candles (his lucky number) and the entire dining car singing Happy Birthday to him. I can still see the joy it brought to his eyes.

After dinner we continued to the piano bar in another car, singing songs like "New York, New York" and "My Way" with the other passengers until the wee hours of the morning. It was truly an unforgettable birthday party.

Watching the countryside go by from the stately and elegant train gave us the feeling of being transported to an era of timeless beauty and exquisite service. As the stunning train climbed the Alps, we watched children play in small Alpine Villages. We exited the train on one stop to take photos and almost missed getting back on board in time!

We arrived in Venice a few days later, and the water taxi brought us to our hotel perched on the main canal. It had old-world charm and we were intrigued by the ambience. When the bellman brought us to our room, there were beautiful flowers and a card.

"Bon journo, me amoura, Jack."

He'd really gone to a lot of trouble to orchestrate all the thoughtful romantic surprises, and I really appreciated his kindness.

My dad and I walked around the canals and I negotiated a gondola ride with a singing gondolier. Yes, he had to sing "O Solo Mia." (I paid extra for that!) What laughs we shared as he sang and paddled us through the narrow canals.

The next morning a stunning, polished teak motorboat was docked outside our hotel. A man approached us and asked if we would like to go to the famous Murano Glass Factoria. We gladly jumped on the gorgeous boat for the short ride to the Factoria where we were greeted warmly by a guy dressed in Italian finery with a plumed hat. He escorted us inside where a demonstration of glassblowing was about to begin. The glassblower delicately blew a small glass horse that looked like a prancing Ferrari horse. It was amazing. Then the salesman arrived and took us into the showroom, pointing out very ornate chandeliers and breathing down my father's neck trying to get him to buy something.

Suddenly my dad said, "Whatever my baby wants, she can have."

Then the guy was all over me like a flea on a monkey. I gave my father a "thanks a lot" eye roll and proceeded to tell this pushy salesman that I had a Southwestern-style home and chandeliers just didn't fit my decor. My protests definitely got lost in translation. To the dismay of the salesman, all I really wanted was the little prancing horse that the glassblower had made earlier. Dad bought the little horse and the disappointed salesman made us leave through the back door and take the public water taxi back to the hotel. We laughed all the way back!

Our final day in Venice happened to be the day of the Kentucky Derby in the United States. My dad and I always had a bet on the derby. So, we went in search of a big-screen television in bars along the waterfront, but there were no big-screen televisions in Venice, and no one knew or cared about the Kentucky Derby.

Finally, we gave up looking and planted ourselves in a little bistro café where we ordered a bottle of Italian wine and some cheese and talked about life. I told my dad that I really wanted to get married again and have him walk me down the aisle at the Wayfarers Chapel in Rancho Palos Verdes, California. At that moment, we both spotted a large white standard-size poodle taking a huge dump on the sidewalk some twenty feet away. The unconcerned owner trotted on and left the mess in the middle of the walkway. The tourists were trying to avoid stepping in the pile.

My dad wagered, "I'll bet you one hundred dollars that a woman steps in it."

I said, "You're on! I'll take a guy!"

So, there we sat screaming and laughing while we watched people sidestep the treacherous pile. One man was hugging and kissing a woman as he approached the pile and I thought for sure I'd win the hundred dollars. At the last second, though, the woman tickled him, and he missed the pile by a fraction of an inch. No one had a clue why we were laughing. Life seemed so simple that day.

I've heard it said that no one, at the end of their life, ever muses, "I wish I'd worked more." Lots of folks, though, harbor regret that they didn't invest more time in the people in their lives.

For years, I'd been prioritizing my career. That's not to say that I let relationships slide. I'd made every effort in my marriage and had nurtured some good friendships. But I'll be the first to admit that work got an awful lot of my time and energy. When Sean left our marriage, a bit of space opened up in my life. And while I could have filled it all kinds of ways, I will always be grateful for having spent that time with my dear father.

If there's a dream in your heart that you're pursuing, it's likely that it gets a lot of your time, energy, and even dollars. And to be fair, that might be necessary. But it's also important to invest in the relationships in your life. That might be a spouse, a child, or a parent. Maybe you've been overworking and have let your friendships slide. Or it might be that the only relationships in your life are with people who are a lot like you, and you have an interest in broadening your circles. I encourage you to spend the time, energy—and even dollars!—to prioritize the relationships you want to nurture. I promise you will *not* regret it.

As my dad and I nibbled on dessert, I asked him what I should do about Jack.

"Follow your heart," he advised, "and don't look back. Maybe it's not in the cards for you to have a kid."

Darkness began to fall as a woman approached the pile while talking to a friend.

"Okay, she's going to nail it," my dad chuckled.

"Oops, looks like she grazed over it. Let's go inspect." I insisted.

We examined the pile and determined it was untouched and a draw. We laughed all the way back to the hotel.

That trip of a lifetime was the most amazing time that I ever spent with my dad. The joy that we experienced was unforgettable.

Because my dad had always taught me to follow my dreams and believe in myself, I was beyond thrilled to make one of his dreams come true, too.

Doing my first real stunt job in a traffic safety film
Getting hit by a car!

Leading the pack racing my Ferrari
Willow Springs International Motorsports Park

King Kong
Doubling Jessica Lange

***Allan Quatermain and the Lost City of Gold* with Richard Chamberlain**
Telling him he was the first person I ever had a crush on

Drag racing my 2000 'Vette
Centerville Drag Strip, Centerville, Arkansas. I won the class!

My Dad's Mack truck
I learned to drive 18-wheelers on it!

Grand Theft Auto
Climbing out of car after demolition derby

***Magnum, P.I.* with Tom Selleck**
That is not my hair! Ha! I did a car chase with the Ferrari in an episode where the Ferrari was stolen by a woman.

***Stir Crazy*, the TV show**
Taking a car into a lake. It was sinking fast!

Massarati and the Brain
I shattered my heel in five places on this fall. Ouch!

Feds **doubling Rebecca De Mornay**
Rappelling down a fifty-foot tower

Father Dowling Mysteries **doubling Tracy Nelson**
Escaping from the bad guys

Feds
Crashing through a window

Bunny Diane
In London and New Jersey

River of Death
Me as a pirate preparing for the huge explosion

***The Laundromat* with Meryl Streep**
After the boat capsized

My horse Tiny Tim

Hi-Riders
Ramp jump through window

Hi-Riders
Starring Diane Peterson

The Hidden
Crashing a Cadillac through the storefront window

Dewar's ad

Grand Theft Auto
Driving Rolls-Royce in a chase

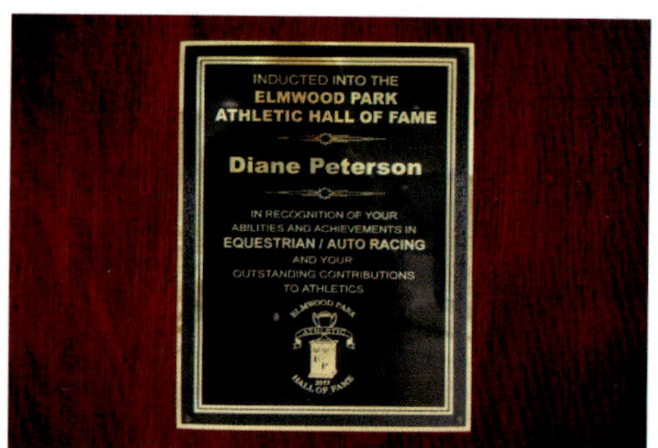

Athletic Hall of Fame
Inducted 2017, Elmwood Park, New Jersey

Rock Explosion
Album cover with brother's Triumph

The Red Bag of Courage
On my Stuntwomen's Association director's chair

Kade the Clydesdale
Elmwood Park Centennial Parade

Smokey
My favorite pony

Walker, Texas Ranger
With Chuck Norris

John Peterson
Best Dad ever!

Death Wish 4: The Crackdown
With Charles Bronson

Arlington Road
With Jeff Bridges

Swimming in the ocean with horse
Mexico

***Miami* Magazine**
Cover

Ready for action on the Suzuki

My 1968 'Vette

Practicing camel riding in Egypt

Having a picnic in Vermont
My brother, Dr. John M. Peterson, and my Mom & Dad, John & Ann Peterson

25

Say Goodbye to Hollywood

When I arrived home from Europe, Jack asked me to marry him.

I said yes immediately, and I began to plan the wedding. I was hoping to get married just six months later because I really wanted my dad to walk me down the aisle and I was becoming concerned about his health. I'd dreamed of getting married at the Wayfarers Chapel in Rancho Palos Verdes for a long time. The small glass and natural wood chapel, surrounded by lush greenery and overlooking the Pacific Ocean, was a magical place. The church was the Swedenborgian Church and came with a minister. Being Catholic, I needed to not only get permission to get married outside the Catholic Church, but also permission to marry a Jew. Having chosen May 18 to be our wedding date, I contacted the local diocese and started the petition. We were required to take an all-day seminar given by the Catholic Church to explore our values and seek answers to the questions that the future might present. I asked my dear friend Reverend J. Patrick

Kelly, a Franciscan priest, if he would officiate at the wedding. He had met and liked Jack and, after all, he had my account, having officiated at my first marriage.

I found a sexy, short white wedding dress adorned with beads and sequins that had a long detachable train. Booking rooms in the Marina Del Rey Hotel for out-of-town guests, I also reserved a yacht for our reception and booked a keyboard player for the party.

Six months flew by amazingly fast!

There was one last-minute red flag when Jack insisted that I sign a prenuptial agreement before the wedding. Though it was very awkward, and I felt pressured into signing, I believed that we would be married forever so it really didn't matter anyway. On the morning of my wedding, May 18, 1995, I felt ready for a new life to begin. I loved this man and was willing and ready to spend the rest of my life with him. We climbed in the white limousine and were whisked off to the Wayfarers Chapel. After signing the obligatory wedding documents, I retired to the bride's chambers to don my gown and put finishing touches on my hair and make-up. Dana, my best friend, was there helping me get ready and calming my nerves. Finally, the time arrived, and I was escorted to the chapel by my dad who looked so happy and handsome in his tuxedo. We walked into the chapel as the string violinist was playing the wedding march.

My dad proudly walked me down the aisle past a church full of well-wishing friends and family. I saw Jack from afar and he was wearing a yarmulke. I was surprised, as he never mentioned that he would be wearing one. As I approached him, I noticed he was in a full sweat mode with perspiration dripping down his face. I smiled and held his hand while the minister began the service. Father Jim and the rent-a-Rabbi were standing on each side of the minister, and each had their part in the ceremony. It was an amazing celebration of three different approaches to the sacred vows of matrimony. After saying our I dos, Jack kissed me, signaling that we were husband and wife and were to live happily ever after. At least that's how the story should go.

Our unique reception on a yacht in Marina Del Rey was a blast. We drank, ate, and danced as the yacht toured the marina. Before the evening ended, we released doves and made a wish for everlasting love. Later that night, Jack and I took off for our honeymoon in Tahiti. Our love story was off and running in what felt like a magical way.

I'd decided that I would sell my house in Simi Valley and really make the commitment to my marriage and my new husband by moving to Plano, Texas, which was not a small sacrifice. However, I was in love and willing to make necessary adjustments to my life for the good of our life together. He was a dentist and didn't want to start his practice all over again in California, which I understood. I figured that I could work anywhere, and I already had a semi-steady job on *Walker, Texas Ranger* in Dallas.

The day the movers came to my home, I wept. I cried for the unfulfilled dreams I'd planted in that house that never came to fruition. I cried for the unborn babies that I'd dreamed of raising there, and I cried because I was saying goodbye to Hollywood. The life I'd built around my Hollywood career would now be a distant memory. To soothe myself, though, I rationalized that I wasn't giving up my dream of being a stuntwoman, I was just changing locations.

I boarded the plane at the Burbank airport, tears running down my face, with the song "Say Goodbye to Hollywood" replaying over and over again in my head. The flight attendant asked me if I was okay, and I just nodded yes and dried my tears with my well-worn tissue.

Embarking on a completely new chapter in my life, I was excited with thoughts of the future. I knew that my new husband loved me and that was all that mattered to me at that moment in time.

Although I'd visited, Texas was still a culture shock. My favorite local expression was, "I'm fixin' to do it." That could mean in an hour or in a week. Jack bought a huge, newly constructed brick house situated on a creek that I'd picked out. My task was to oversee the creation of another boulder swimming pool with a diving rock similar to the pool I'd had designed for my home in Simi Valley. Picking out where each and every boulder would be placed, I had fun driving the heavy equipment around the massive backyard overlooking the creek from a cliff. The finished product was a unique masterpiece with a waterfall and hot tub designed to exactly fit our bodies.

I worked feverishly to get a new agent and make some other television and film contacts. I loved working on *Walker, Texas Ranger*, but I longed for other jobs to keep me busy. Though I missed being close to the ocean, we went on numerous trips to the Caribbean to make up for it. Life was good, but a sense of boredom was slowly descending. There was only so much shopping and exploring that I could do in a town with concrete everywhere. And let's talk about the blistering heat. Running from the air-conditioned house to the air-conditioned car was the way of life. Try to golf with ice packs tied around your neck! Sure, there was water. But that meant sweltering on the boat before jumping into the murky, hot lake water filled with tree stumps. Life in Texas was different from anything I'd known.

Feeling like a fish out of water, I'd often think, *What have I done?* My most happy and productive times were working on *Walker*. I was searching for meaning and purpose in my life and was having a challenging time discerning it. Being the doc's wife was not enough for me. Jack tried to get me to work in the office, but that wasn't a good fit. I'd learned that already while working in the dental office in New Jersey! So, in order to help out, I decided to do the weekly Sam's Club run and Staples run for office supplies. I tried to make it fun like a scavenger hunt to amuse myself, but every once in a while, I'd come to the realization that I was just being a gofer.

That didn't sit well in my psyche.

When I tried volunteering at the zoo, the first day was great. They gave me some apples to feed the elephants and a brush to groom the giraffes. The next time, though, they handed me a shovel and pointed me in the direction of the elephant turds. After wheelbarrowing several loads into the dumpster and nearly vomiting, I was then sent to the giraffe pen to rake up their marble-size waste pellets. I was soldiering through it, but the final straw was the hippopotamus pen. I was given a firefighter-type enormous hose to wash down the walls of the hippo pen where the hippo had sprayed liquid excrement. Needless to say, my zoo career came to a screeching halt.

I decided to become a Big Sister, and I was matched up with a ten-year-old little boy from the inner city. I began seeing him once a week, and my life felt like it had special meaning. Some of the best times I had in Dallas were with this little boy whom I loved.

For years I'd yearned to share life with a partner who loved me as much as I loved him. And in Jack I'd finally found that person. Building a life together, however, required me to give up some things, and I was willing to make those sacrifices. I left the home I'd loved. I left friends. I left the geographic hub for the work I adored. And I rooted myself in a new city that felt very foreign to a Jersey girl who'd made California "home."

In some ways, my dreams—of having satisfying work and building a family—competed with one another. And moment by moment, I was trying to make the best decisions I could make to nurture those dreams. In this season of early marriage, I released some of the professional opportunities I was so enjoying for the sake of building a life with Jack.

If you're anything like me, you may have several dreams vying for your time and energy. Whether your goals are related to career, relationships, health, or something else, you may find, in a particular season, that they tug against one another. The best I could do, and the best you can do, is to notice the pull and adjust—release what you're being called to release, and embrace what you're being called to embrace.

As I started my marriage to Jack, I felt that tug. And each day, I did the best I could to be a good wife.

Because Teddy's still had my number, I received a call for my availability to fly to Mexico and work on the film *Titanic* for a few weeks. I talked with Jack and told him that I'd really like to work on this project. We had accepted the invitation to be Mr. and Mrs. Santa Claus at the neighborhood Christmas party, and he graciously agreed to be Santa Claus alone. It was difficult leaving because we were newlyweds, but I knew an opportunity like this wouldn't come along very often. So, I prepared to leave the country for an incredible journey into the first-class filmmaking that I loved so much.

The stunt crew was sequestered in a Taj Mahal-type hotel in Rosarito Beach, Mexico. I was flown into San Diego first class from Dallas and driven across the border in a van packed with other eager stuntmen and women from around the world. Our stunt bags were jammed into the overcrowded bus, and my Red Bag of Courage was perched on top of the pile. I always kept an eye on my Red Bag of Courage because without it my body would be toast.

It's funny that in the early days of doing stunts, I would say, "That's okay, I don't need any pads," because I really didn't want to look fat in the wardrobe. Now, years later, I used all the padding that I could get away with, not caring about the visuals and only concerned with my safety and comfort. Wisdom comes with age.

We reached the Taj Mahal-looking hotel, and I was escorted to my modest, white, tidy room with the million-dollar view of the turquoise ocean where I would spend the next several weeks. The script read that "it was a calm night," but in reality, that seldom happened during the shoot. The El Norte winds were blowing a mean streak.

Upon arrival, the stunt crew was quickly ushered into a huge ballroom and the director, James Cameron, made an appearance. He informed us that for the next three days, we would be watching documentaries of the ship sinking and getting wardrobe, hair, and makeup set. Three days to watch movies of a sinking ship and getting paid?! How cool is that?

Cameron said he wanted us to get a good feel for what really happened to the folks on the *Titanic* that fateful night. James was a perfectionist, and we had no idea of the enormity of this film. Frankly, when I read the script, I didn't think it was going to be a blockbuster by any means at all.

In the wardrobe department, I started trying on all kinds of cool period costumes. I didn't want one of those tight corseted dresses where I wouldn't be able to hide pads, so I opted for an elegant black dress with a gray cashmere overcoat. I could hide lots of lifesaving pads under that stylish coat. They also fitted me with an enormous, beautiful hat that looked like a flying saucer perched on my head. Black hose and lace-up boots completed my look, and I was then off to hair and makeup. I tried on a series of hideous wigs and finally found one that was kind of cute in an old-fashioned way. Brown, curly, short hair was my new look, with ghostly white makeup. I was sporting a tan, so the makeup artist had her work cut out for her. Tons of white pancake makeup, exceptionally light eyeliner, and merlot lips! I was ready to hit the deck.

At our first rehearsal, we were sitting in the lifeboats, suspended high above the ocean, waiting to be rescued before the ship sank. There were about eighteen of us packed like sardines into the tiny rescue boat. They began to lower the boat, men shouting orders, as one side dipped, and we all screamed and slid sideways. The stunt man sitting across from me was from the Czech Republic and didn't speak much English. Devilishly handsome and built like a strong bull, he was wearing a jacket with something written on the outside of his jacket under his name.

When we had a break, I asked Igor, "What is that written under you name?"

He growled, "Blood type!"

Oh my God, I thought. *I don't want to sit near him. He's an accident waiting to happen!* Why in the world would anyone have their blood type written on the outside of their jacket? Thinking that he was very accident prone, I adjusted my seating position!

Rehearsing the scene repeatedly, with the lifeboats going up and down on the hoists, we, the passengers, were nearly falling out of the boats to a death plunge in the icy, cold sea. Finally darkness fell, and it was time to begin shooting the scene. It took five hours to get the hundreds of atmosphere (extra background) passengers ready with wardrobe, wigs, and makeup. We boarded the ship and took our places in the lifeboats, and the mighty El

Norte winds began to blow. "It was a calm night" echoed in my brain as the ship shook and swayed.

James Cameron, looking completely frazzled, yelled, "That's a wrap. Everyone exit the ship quickly."

I thought the ship was going to collapse. After all, it was only a facade. The single freight-type elevator was jammed with extras, and my dear friend Dana said, "Let's get outta here!" and she began climbing down the rafters some fifty feet above the pavement below. I gingerly followed her down because the heels of my boots were getting caught in the hem of my long coat—a flashback to *King Kong* days! The idea of the ship collapsing was enough to motivate me to keep scrambling down like a little monkey. Not a bit of filming was accomplished that night.

The El Norte winds lingered on for weeks, making filming difficult and adding to the huge budget of the glorious *Titanic*. We eventually got the enormous scene shot with the hoists getting jammed and people nearly falling out of the life rafts. I couldn't help but imagine the peril of the passengers of that fateful night when the *Titanic* sank.

When the film was released, we were invited to the screening at 20th Century Fox lot in Los Angeles where there was a huge replica of the ship with smoke coming out of the smokestacks. We watched in awe as the story unfolded into one of the most fantastic movies that I ever had the pleasure of working on. I still get residuals from that amazing film!

26

Unraveling

As time went on in our marriage, the amount of alcohol Jack and I drank increased dramatically. Guess I could blame it on the frequent vacations we took, but the daily use at home escalated to epic proportions. I could blame it on boredom, or me missing California, but the bottom line was that alcohol began to interfere with everyday life, and I was beginning to fear succumbing to the grip of alcoholism. After all, it ran in my family. My uncle Carl was a mess of a drunk. When I was seven years old and my grandfather died, Uncle Carl was riding in the back seat of my dad's car on the way to the funeral with me and my brother.

He smelled stinky as he talked to me and he whispered in my ear, "Grandpa's only sleeping."

When we arrived at the funeral home, I walked over to the coffin and shook my grandpa's arm to wake him up. He was stiff as a board! I took off terrified, screaming and crying. That shock stayed with me for years to come. Even now, I have a challenging time dealing with funeral services.

Wanting to get a handle on my alcohol consumption, I decided to go for a five-day detox at a local institution in the Dallas area. My counselor had cautioned me that both Jack and I needed to quit drinking together or it wouldn't work. I knew that Jack wasn't willing to quit, and he pretended that alcohol was only my problem, not his. My counselor wasn't wrong: I only stayed sober for the obligatory thirty days after the program and soon fell back into the pattern of daily drinking and passing out at night with Jack. Vacations became drinking festivals day and night, and it was beginning to wear me down. We had more frequent fights about nothing, or sometimes we couldn't remember what we'd even been fighting about the following day. Even that was not enough for him to join me in rejecting the insidious poison that plagued us both.

I noticed that I was having trouble remembering simple things from the night before as well as feeling absolutely horrible and shaky in the mornings. Although I knew I needed to go back to detox and clean up my act, I still had no support from my husband. Time and time again, he continued to drink in front of me when I was trying to stay sober. Eventually, I began to despise his drinking. I fought to stay sober for an entire year, which wasn't easy. But after a year, I thought I was better and that I could control the monster within that forced me to overindulge.

So, on a vacation in the Caribbean when I was watching Jack drink, I said, "I want one of those drinks with the umbrella in it," and Jack immediately ordered it for me.

I was back at the races in no time. Only this time it was worse. It seemed that by not drinking for a year, the alcohol took effect more quickly and damaged my ability to think straight. I wanted to believe it was a temporary setback, and that I would soon be able to resume my normal overindulging and be able to handle it, but I couldn't. And I was scared, very scared.

When I started drinking again, I began to give away my power. Normally I was a strong, decisive, well-organized example of womanhood. But when the alcohol kicked in, slowly but surely, I'd lose all the characteristics that made me the outstanding lady who I was created to be.

Knowing I had to take control and quit drinking once and for all, I checked into a thirty-day treatment center in Arizona called The Meadows in the middle of nowhere in Wickenburg, Arizona. Jack was accompanying me to Arizona, and he got drunk the morning that we were going to the airport. He was unwilling to join me in the program but agreed to help me arrive there safely. Because I had a broken leg from falling in the backyard, he dropped me at the curb outside the terminal, with wheelchair and crutches, while he went to park the car. Forgetting where he had left me, I sat there for a very long time. Finally, asking someone for help, I was wheeled to the gate. I was determined to get well with or without him.

About five minutes before the plane was to take off, Jack came stumbling onto the plane and drank the rest of the way to Arizona. A driver picked us up at the airport and drove us to The Meadows where I had to give up my cell phone and say goodbye to Jack. I was happy to say goodbye to him because his behavior was so obnoxious that it made me sick to my stomach. He bought me a teddy bear from the gift shop, but he didn't offer me any encouragement and disappeared quickly. I felt so sad and alone, but I was on a mission to get well and gain my power back.

That week I fully embraced the intense work of examining my past and delving into the root of my disease. It was difficult and painful, both mentally and physically, especially being on crutches and in a wheelchair.

But I made my way and did my work as told.

When I called Jack one night he said, "Don't ever call me again, you are like a tumor that I have to get rid of."

The words cut like a knife. Thank God, the wise counselors aided me in my distress. I could still not believe that he could be so cruel and uncaring. When I saw others laughing with genuine real laughter, I knew I wanted some of that, too. I committed myself to learning, studying, examining my life, and staying sober. During family week, all the other patients had their spouses or children come to participate in the exercises and support them. Jack, however, refused to come. He might have had to stay sober for a few days himself, and that was something he could not or would not do. So, I sat alone, and vowed to stay sober one day at a time. My birthday came, and he didn't even call or send me a card or flowers, which felt so cruel. I was trying to get better, and he did everything he could to make me feel worse.

My dear brother John was the only one who came to visit me. He flew all the way out to Arizona from Vermont to see me for one day when visitors were permitted. He gave me the hope and encouragement that I so desperately needed. I am so thankful for the long journey he took to visit me and give me support.

When it was time for graduation and the accompanying desert trip, there was a discussion that I might not be able to take the desert excursion because of my crutches. But I insisted that I wanted to go, and I'm so glad I did. As the sun was setting in an intense orange, hot-pink sky, I asked God to please take away the alcohol obsession that I had developed. Ask and you shall receive. It has been over fifteen years since that day that I will never forget and I am forever grateful to The Meadows and all my counselors there and to my sponsor, Lis, back in Plano, Texas. Most of all, I thank God for answering my prayers.

Now I had to return home and face an unloving, uncaring jerk. He had my neighbor and best friend, Babe, pick me up at the airport and I stayed at her house across the street until he decided that I could come back home. It was so awful that I really don't know how I made it. I was determined to be strong, though, to carry on and not drink.

Once I was back in the house of hell, I hated every minute of being with him. Unloving, uncaring, and rude, he got drunk every night, making living with him a total nightmare.

I knew I needed to step back into my own power, overcome my fear of being an alcoholic, and just stay sober. Slowly I gathered strength as I gained clarity about the situation. My resolve was about to be tested.

"Open the goddamn door!" Jack screamed, pounding on the door between us.

Sitting up in the guest room bed, startled, I looked at the clock. Three o'clock in the morning. Why was he banging on the door of the guest room now? *Bam! Bam! Bam!*

"Open the fucking door, you bitch!" he hollered.

I clutched my bull terrier, Mack, and prayed that Jack would go away. He was so drunk earlier in the evening that I'd locked myself and my dog in the guest room, and now there was no way to escape.

After locking the adjoining bathroom door, I heard him trying the doorknob and screaming, "Let me in, let me in! Now!"

Does he have his gun that he keeps in the nightstand?

Frightening thoughts raced through my head. Would this be the end that I was praying for? I didn't want my life to end this way. Did he have a sharp kitchen knife to slit my throat? Would he even remember the terror he was inflicting on me the next day? Earlier that evening, Jack had a handful of my gold jewelry and threatened to throw it in the creek below our home on the hill. When I tried to grab the jewelry from him, he pushed me hard. Because I didn't want to get into a physical fight with a 210-pound drunk maniac, I ran and got Mack and beelined to the guest bedroom. Now I lay there looking at the door and shaking.

"Leave me alone," I said with all the courage I could muster, "or I'm going to call the police."

"Open the fucking door, you bitch," he growled.

I made believe that I was calling 911.

"Operator," I spoke loudly enough for Jack to hear, "my husband is trying to break into my room and I'm afraid he's going to hurt me."

If I really called 911 and he got arrested, I knew that it would be the end of our marriage. Praying in the midst of the terror, I asked God if this was the sign that I was looking for. Finally, there was silence outside the door. I thought, *Oh God, maybe he will leave me alone*. Though I tried to go back to sleep, I could only lay there wishing and praying that the nightmare of this marriage would end. I didn't know the demon who lived inside the man I once loved so much. The booze and pills had contorted Jack's mind, heart, and soul, unleashing the monster lurking within. His mind had disintegrated like flesh in acid, and his heart had hardened like concrete.

Suddenly, I heard the sound of a screwdriver.

Oh God!

The maniac was trying to take the doorknob off! This was the sign from God that I had been waiting for. With what felt like a small window to escape from hell, it was suddenly crystal clear what I needed to do.

I called the police.

"Operator," I explained frantically, "I'm locked in a bedroom and my drunk husband is trying to take the doorknob off. I'm afraid he is going to kill me."

Just then I heard Jack yell, "I'm going to wreck your car!"

"Operator," I reported, "he said he was going to wreck my car!"

"Please don't leave the room until the police get there," the operator firmly instructed.

I had hidden the keys to my precious Ferrari because I thought Jack might destroy the car I loved, but my Corvette keys remained on the hook.

Minutes seemed like hours as I waited to be rescued. When the doorbell rang, I bolted to the door.

One of the two police officers asked, "What's going on here?"

Just then the monster raced out of the driveway in my red Corvette.

"That's my husband," I reported, "he's drunk, and he said he's going to wreck my car!"

The police darted down the walkway, jumped into their car, and took off screeching after him. Shaking terribly, I immediately called my dear, sweet neighbor and best friend, Babe.

"Babe," I said breathlessly, "the police just came and are chasing Jack in my Corvette. Please come over quick!"

Throwing on her robe, Babe ran across the street and hugged me tight as I cried and cried. I knew if I called the police, I would be in serious trouble with the wreck of a human being with whom I shared a life. But I knew I could no longer live in terror.

In my kitchen, Babe made us some tea and offered, "You can stay at my house."

It's what I'd often done to find refuge from the chaos in my own home.

Fear had replaced trust and love, and the man I once knew was but a shell of his former self. The loving, caring, trustworthy, fun, sexy man who I married had evaporated into thin air. There was now a look of evil that I never knew was dwelling behind those penetrating blue eyes that I once loved.

When the doorbell rang, I was afraid to answer it. Peeking through the peephole in the door, though, I could see that the police were back.

When I opened the door they said, "We chased your husband for a few blocks, and he finally pulled over. He was so drunk he could barely stand. We arrested him, and we suggest that you do not be here when he gets out of jail. He is one terribly angry man."

"Wh-when is he getting out?" I stammered.

One of the officers explained, "When you bail him out."

Without hesitation I announced, "I'm not bailing him out."

"When the judge gets in in the morning, he will be able to call his lawyer and post bail. Why don't you leave for a few days till things cool down? Come on, we'll give you a ride to your car. We didn't have it towed away. He's lucky he didn't kill someone tonight."

Babe and I literally fell into the back seat of the cop car. It was a low, bare plastic seat for criminals who puked and peed on the way to the slammer.

When we got to my car they advised, "Be careful around that guy, he's dangerous."

Back at the house, I began packing like a madwoman. Feeling as if my house was on fire, I picked my favorite possessions so that I could get the hell out! I filled my Ferrari with clothes and meaningful remnants of my life that I knew Jack would destroy to get even, regardless of whether he was drunk or not. I drove my Ferrari to the dealer's lot where I knew that I could store my car. Then Babe drove me back to the cold, brick shell of a house that I used to call home. I gathered my dog's bowls, bed, toys, and cookies and filled my Corvette to the brim with everything that I could grab that was precious to me. Mack was by my side constantly, sensing my distress and remaining calm in the mist of the chaos.

The phone rang at six o'clock in the morning.

"Bitch," Jack blasted, "I got arrested last night! You bitch, when are you coming to get me?!"

Click. I hung up the phone. I wasn't going to pick him up or be home when he got out. And I wasn't going to let him talk to me like that ever again. Babe got on the computer and found me a place to stay that would accept my dog. I didn't dare stay across the street at her house. I booked a room under an assumed name so he couldn't find me at the hotel.

Frightened for my life, I gave Babe a big hug, and sobbing, I picked up Mack, hopped in my car, and headed down the road to another life that lay ahead. The taste of my heartbreak was bitter. After arriving at my hideaway, I got into my room and felt a profound sense of relief. I was free from the chains that bound me to a man whom I once adored. Now, though, he was the devil in disguise. The hatred was crusted so thick around his heart that he could no longer feel the love we once shared.

I had to make a plan. I called an attorney who I'd talked to a few times before when things were getting really bad at home. She told me that she was worried about me and that I didn't deserve to live like that. Knowing she was right, I made an appointment to see her the next day.

When I walked into her office, she hugged me and told me that she was glad I was safe.

After I reported the gruesome story of what happened, she said, "I've got a funny feeling about this."

She began typing on her computer.

"Aha," she said, "he filed for divorce this morning."

He was a coward and could never face the fact that he was a drunk and needed help. I was done with him and needed to leave the drinking life and him behind. My attorney advised me to stay away from him for good. I was advised by her to remain in Texas for six months until the divorce was final.

The following Sunday, when I was in church, I thought about the marriage vows I'd made and took seriously. I decided to wait until the afternoon and go over to our house with a pamphlet from a counselor that I had gone to see. He specialized in addictions and relationships that were affected by this dreaded disease.

I opened the door to our house that now felt like a mausoleum. It stank of stale booze and cigarettes, and I found Jack passed out drunk on the couch. I snapped a few photos of him to remind me of the disgusting pig that I used to live with and left the pamphlet on the countertop with a note.

"Dear Jack, let's get some help. I still love you, Diane."

Did I? Were the words empty? Did I want to try again for the sake of our marriage vows? Maybe he would see the light.

It didn't take too long before he called me and answered. "Fuck you. I want to go down smoking and drinking." Well, have at it . . .

At every tricky turn in our relationship, I'd done what I knew how to do. And now I was at the end of what I knew to do. The Alcoholics Anonymous serenity prayer exhorts, "God grant me the serenity to accept the things I cannot change, the courage to change the things I can, and the wisdom to know the difference." At that point in my life, God was granting me the wisdom to know the difference.

I'd changed what I could change: I'd gotten sober.

And I was accepting the fact that what I could not change was . . . Jack.

God was helping me let go of what I could not change.

Jack and I had shared a number of very good years together and I'm grateful for that. The fact that he would choose booze over us was both baffling and heartbreaking. I knew that I was being called once again to follow the dream that I'd given up for a life with him in Texas. Strong and confident, I knew that I could be happy again and live the life I always imagined. I had to get back home to LA, the sooner the better.

27

Home Sweet Home, LA

As I was preparing to make my move back to Los Angeles, my answering service called to find out if I was available for two weeks of work in Los Angeles on a film called Super Hero. The request was an answer to my prayer and an affirmation that that LA was calling me home. What I most needed was to get away, try to rebuild my career, and mend my shattered heart. It felt like divine providence that stunt coordinator Charlie Croughwell called me to work.

I had worked with Charlie on a few movies over the years, and now I was thrilled to be going back to Los Angeles, the place I loved most, and to be working again on a feature film. Sometimes the universe knows exactly what you need at the exact moment you need it. I knew it was a God thing for sure.

My first priority was to find a kennel where I could hide Mack so that Jack couldn't find him. Once before, he'd taken my dog and put him in a kennel and wouldn't tell me where he was.

When said he was going to sell my Mack, I believed him. How cruel could one be? Unable to bear the thought of losing my best friend, I wouldn't let that happen again. I located a rural kennel in the outskirts of Dallas where I felt comfortable leaving Mack, giving strict orders to the staff that under no circumstances could Mack be released to anyone other than me. My friend Babe was the only other person who knew where he was, and she was the only person on his guest list. Swearing her to secrecy, I was confident I could trust her. The day I took Mack to the kennel, I cried. He'd been my faithful and true companion through the lonely nights in my new little apartment that I'd moved to while waiting for the divorce. I hugged him and told him not to worry, and that I would be back.

All I knew about the stunt job was that it was going to be a huge fight scene, which was always a ton of fun. Returning to the set at 20th Century Fox was truly like a homecoming. So many of my stunt buddies were there, all happy to see me. Vince Deadrick Jr., with whom I'd worked with so many times before, had a broad smile and gave me a big bear hug. Melting into his arms, I felt I was home at last. Little did Charlie know how much this job meant to me. It reinforced my sense of self-worth and reassured me that there would be a future once again for me doing my dream job in Los Angeles. I'd been away for ten long years, which was much *too* long.

I got called to wardrobe to be fitted in party clothes because the scene was taking place in a huge ballroom. A fight was scheduled to break out between about seventy-five background actors and about thirty stuntmen and stuntwomen. The background actors were placed around tables between the stunt people's tables. Fitted in a pretty blue flowing dress with rhinestones, I was grateful to have a wardrobe that I could really move around in and even hide a few small stunt pads.

On action, a fight erupted from the front of the ballroom after Leslie Nielson told a dirty joke on stage. Vince ran to get into the fight. I took off after him and jumped on his back. He whirled me around as I was kicking people over with my legs. Suddenly, a woman grabbed me by the hair and yanked me off Vince's back. After punching her in the stomach, she kicked me in the knee. Falling down, she jumped on me, and we rolled around in a catfight until a guy tried to break us apart. Then we both started to beat him up! By this time, the entire ballroom was in a frenzy. Chairs and tables were flying, and glass was breaking, sounding like the biggest barroom brawl ever! The background actors were running and screaming and told to stay out of our way. My joy was back! My dream in gear again, I felt so alive and full of hope for the future.

This one fight scene took about a week to shoot. The choreography of the fight was like a delicate ballet until "action" was spoken. Then all hell broke loose as we all tried to follow the basic plan. But something unexpected always happens. Sometimes someone falls before it's their turn to go down; an extra might get in the way and hit the deck; a heel could break on a shoe. But the fight continues, and we all improvise until we hear the magic word: cut. There is always camera coverage from all angles, wide shots, close-ups, and nonstop fun for all of us. There was no doubt that I would be sore at the end of the day from being tossed around and bouncing off tables, chairs, and the floor, but the physical pain was a delightful diversion from the mental anguish I'd been going through.

In Texas, as I mentioned, it takes six months from when you file for divorce to actually finalizing the divorce. So, I had to go back to purgatory until the waiting period was up. Six months seemed like six million years, but I kept reminding myself, "One day at a time."

Truly happy again, I rekindled friendships that had been long neglected by my absence from Los Angeles. And I was energized by following the dream that I had put on the back burner.

When the shoot ended, I took a few days to explore Malibu. I knew that the divorce was imminent, and I'd always wanted to live by the sea. In my imagination I would wake up and see the sun rise over the ocean. Driving up and down the little streets near the beach, I tried visualizing my new life. Wandering down a tiny private road called Latigo Shore, I noticed a condominium complex. There was a unit with a for sale sign on it that was situated directly on the oceanfront. I longed for that spot to be my home, but I wasn't ready to move yet. Plus, I had no idea how much this perfectly placed nest by the sea would cost.

I returned to Dallas and went straight to the kennel to wrap my arms around my faithful friend, Mack. Spinning around, he was so happy to see me. We went directly home to my tiny one-bedroom apartment overlooking a parking lot. It was a peaceful haven, in sharp contrast to the house of hell I'd left behind.

There was a trio of pine trees on a vacant lot beyond the parking lot that I'd imagine to be the vast ocean, and I would hear the waves crashing on the beach. Holding onto my vision made the days bearable until my exit. My focus was on the future as I dealt with the legalities that were forced upon me. Mediation, court dates, and countless money spent on attorney's fees. But I knew that soon, I would be free.

About a month before I was ready to move, I looked online in the Malibu Times newspaper and found a two-line advertisement: Condo for rent, oceanfront, Tivoli Cove, and a phone number. I called and talked to John, the son of the man who owned the condo, and told him that I would be there the next day to look at the place. I asked him to please wait to until I saw it before he rented it to anyone else, assuring him that I had excellent credit. I also found one other unit for rent at Tivoli Cove. When I arrived the next day, I went to the other unit first. It was quite lovely and had a great ocean view from the living room. The bedroom had a view of the red rooftop of the building in front of it which I didn't like at all. Also, the parking spaces were exposed near the garage entrance in the subterranean parking.

Next, I marched to see the unit that I originally called about and met John. Lo and behold it was the unit I'd seen months earlier from the street that was for sale! I'd envisioned living there for months. When I walked in, it immediately felt like home. John explained that the condo was for sale for $865,000, or for rent at $2,800 a month. Without a job I was in no position to buy the place.

So I said, "I'll take it for rent."

I signed all the necessary documents and gave John a deposit check, excited to be so close to living the vision I'd pictured in my head. I was blessed.

After flying back to Dallas, I made all the arrangements for my furniture and cars to be shipped. I was moving like a steam engine, canceling my gym membership, giving notice on my apartment, and saying my final goodbyes to friends.

On my final morning in Plano, Texas, I was at Babe's house waiting for the limo to take me to the airport since Babe said it was too sad for her to take me. I understood. I considered saying my last goodbye to Jack. I don't know why but I guess I just needed closure. Calling him one last time, I told him that I was leaving in a few minutes and asked him if he wanted to say goodbye to Mack.

He nastily barked, "I want to say goodbye to you!"

Click!

He was bitter and angry about the divorce that he initiated and inflicted his wrath on me.

I hung up the phone, and that was the last time I ever talked to him. Thank God.

I flew into Los Angeles, hopped in my rental car, and drove to Malibu. It was April 27, 2008. April 27 was my dad's birthday, and I felt that it was an excellent sign that the moving van was scheduled to arrive later that day. Sadly, my beloved parents had passed away several years before. I was more than ready to begin my new life in my sweet, little condo by the sea. My new place fulfilled the three requirements I had in a home: I could see and hear the ocean; it had safe and secure parking for my Ferrari and Corvette; it was a dog-friendly environment.

Mack was afraid to go too close to the ocean. Jack used to throw him in the pool, and he was terrified of water. I knew that I'd need to take baby steps to get Mack accustomed to the ocean and the mighty waves. I'd never force him and just gently nudge him closer until he realized that the beach was fun.

Securing Mack in the condo, I went for a long walk on the beach. I was feeling deep gratitude to God, thanking Him for bringing me to a place where I could be at peace and live the life I so desperately desired and deserved.

The bumpy path I'd walked over the previous decade was neither the one I'd imagined for myself as a girl nor the one I would have chosen. And I know for sure that God never left me. Throughout my injuries, disappointments, and difficult relationships, God had walked with me. In some moments his presence was obvious to me, and in others I struggled to see him. But feeling the sand and waves under my feet that day, I was certain that God had been with me all along and God would stay with me.

28

Rebuilding My Life

When the Screen Actors Guild went on strike in the late seventies, I decided to get my real estate license to have an income until we went back to work. Deciding that I'd regain my real estate license, I began studying for the exam as my license had long lapsed. I'd always known that I had that career to fall back on when the stunt jobs became fewer and farther between.

Since I'd been out of the Los Angeles film business loop for ten long years, I knew it would take some time to reconnect and establish new contacts. Everything was being done electronically, but luckily, I'd kept up with learning computer skills, so I could dive right in.

I saw an ad in the *Malibu Times* for a local theater company, Malibu Stage Company. I called and arranged a meeting with the artistic director, Richard Johnson. We immediately hit it off, and I became a member of the Zuma Repertory Company. Rick was a bundle of good energy. He stood about five feet nine inches, was in great shape, handsome, with a mop of silver hair and a knack for doing three things at once.

I was thrilled to be back on stage after all those years of being away from it during college. It felt like a wonderful rebirth. I immediately had a newfound family of actor friends close by. And the theater was six minutes from my house!

Rick was producing a show called *Glorious!* although the billboard on Pacific Coast Highway was anything but glorious looking.

When I told him that the sign was boring and uninteresting, he smiled and ordered, "Fix it then!"

I immediately went to the art store and purchased DayGlo paints and proceeded to make the sign look extremely glorious, just like the name of the play. Since Rick knew he could count on me to get things done, I began to produce plays with him. I was willing to do the work in the box office, the sound booth, selling tickets, advertising, helping with casting, and pitching in whenever and wherever I could. I felt connected and useful and excited about using my college degree knowledge in a brand-new environment.

We had a wonderful Monday night scene study. Rick dissected my acting and was brutally honest. I knew that I was rusty, but it was exhilarating to be back onstage and working on my craft. It wasn't long before I got my first role in the production of *I Love You, You're Perfect, Now Change*. I was an angel and the first cast member to appear on stage. The excitement of being in front of a live audience was similar to the rush I felt before a big stunt—that electric feeling that I love so much. I'd found a home at the Malibu Stage Company.

I also connected with old friends and stunt contacts. Dana was happy to have me back in town. I bought a surfboard and a wet suit and began to tackle surfing, something I'd never tried before. She began to teach me surfing, which is much harder than it looks!

I also reconnected with my dear friend Margot, who designed flowers and loved to hike with me. We had such fun catching up and chatting about old times. Being in LA again felt *so right*.

I joined Our Lady of Malibu Catholic Church and met the wonderful pastor there, Father Bill. I volunteered to help where they needed me and soon became a lector for the Mass on Sundays.

I began going to the Ferrari Club of America's monthly board meetings at the Petersen Automotive Museum in Los Angeles and quickly became a board member and then later the president. I organized many Ferrari events and became good friends with many other like-minded car lovers.

One day in early 2009, my agent called out of the blue to ask if I was available to work the next day on a horror movie titled *Children of the Corn: Genesis*. The director was Joel Soisson.

My agent explained, "The director saw your photo and requested you."

"That's great! No audition! I'm in."

I usually had to go to an audition and then have a callback or second audition before booking a job if it were an acting role. This time it was an acting role with a stunt—my favorite combo. My agent described it as "a little fall," no big deal. Because I knew that a stunt could always evolve into something completely unplanned, I still always carried my Red Bag of Courage with all my items of protection.

As soon as I arrived on the set of a spooky-looking old farmhouse, the assistant director spotted me and whisked me to my dressing room. It was wonderful to see my name on the dressing room door once again. He asked me if I'd like something to eat and handed me the contracts that I needed to sign. Because I feel lighter and quicker before eating, I thanked him and said I would pass on the meal. He directed me to go to the hair and makeup trailer when I was ready.

In my dressing room, I noticed a plain-looking house dress with small printed flowers on it. It looked like a dress that an old grandmother would wear. I thought, *That's okay. I'm getting paid and I really don't care what I have to wear or how bad my hair or wig looks*. I'd gotten over that a long time ago. So, I slipped into the homely dress and made sure I could hide my hip pads tucked in the tiny girdle that held them in place. Fortunately, there were low-heeled shoes, almost flats. Now that was one benefit of being older: I no longer had to run around as the hooker in high heels and a miniskirt.

I made my way to the hair trailer and was introduced to my fright wig. No kidding! It was a hideous mess of gray hair that a crazy woman in an asylum might have. After the hairdresser put about a hundred bobby pins in my hair with tight pin curls, she slipped a stocking cap over my skull and plopped the gray nest on my head. Then she began to anchor the nest down with a hundred more bobby pins! This wig was going nowhere.

When I hopped into the makeup chair the makeup artist said apologetically, "I'm so sorry, I have to make you look dead."

"Oh, wonderful! Have at it!" I laughed.

Little by little. my face became a pasty, grayish white. Then came the wrinkles. Deep furrowed laugh lines, rings under my eyes, cracked chapped lips all prepared me to meet the director. I was a frightening sight, but I remained cool, calm, and confident.

When the director was called to the trailer, he took one look at me and said, "She looks too dead, freshen her up a bit."

After a few failed attempts to make me look more "freshly dead," the makeup artist finally got it right and I was approved for the scene. By then, when I was walking around, I could hear comments like, "Gee she looks scary." "What happened to her?" "Yikes!" I just ignored them and began to get into character.

Entering the ominous farmhouse, I was escorted to the living room where trappings of a party were set out. There was a long table filled with freshly baked breads and pies, iced tea, and lemonade. There was a record player playing, just skipping over and over again, stuck in the same place. After the director showed me the wall on which I was to be impaled, the set decorator brought in an apple box for me to stand on. I leaned against the wall with my shoulders slumped, my head hanging down and my arms limp. The director explained that on action, my son, dressed in an army uniform, would enter the house. The scene was supposed to be a homecoming party for him. As he enters the living room and calls for Mom, he notices a strange little evil-looking doll pinned to the wall in front of him. When he grabs the weird, freaky doll, pulling it off the wall, I fall from the wall across the room and hit the floor. He runs to me crying, "Mom, Mom!" as I lie there dead. That was the scene. It took all day to shoot.

One other benefit of being an older stuntwoman was that everyone was extra concerned that I didn't get hurt. First of all, they brought in a huge gym pad for me to fall into. In the rehearsals, I could just fall into the pad, and it was very cushy. The timing was critical so that when he removed the doll, I would fall in sync. And the director was concerned that the fall look like I was a dead limp body.

Although it wasn't easy to do, I did it over and over again. Then they had to take away the crash pad for my close up of hitting the floor. I had my trusty pads on, but hitting the floor is like hitting cement, and it does jar you quite a bit. Unfortunately, the actor playing my son was young and inexperienced, repeatedly made mistakes, and didn't hit his mark. When he ran over to kneel down crying at my side, he kneeled on my hand! I couldn't scream "ouch" because I'd ruin the scene. The next take he tripped over my foot, leaned down, and crushed my boob! This guy was dangerous. I politely told him to get his act together, calm down, and get it right, which he finally did. The director hugged me and told me I was terrific when we finally finished the shoot.

I ran to get the gnarly pins out of my head and the fright wig removed. The makeup man gave me wads of cream to remove the pounds of cake makeup on my face. I returned to the set as the real me and said my goodbyes. I still got some head turns and winks as the real me. After a day of falls, I was feeling sore and was ready for the hot tub when I got home. The business had changed for me in so many ways, but I still loved it.

I began taking a boot camp class at the Bluffs Park, and immediately following that strenuous workout was a yoga class. I had tried yoga before but had never really gotten in the groove. Not only did my yoga instructor have the voice of an angel, grace and kindness exuded from her every pore. I quickly looked forward to her amazing class where we would practice yoga and then end the class with a quiet meditation where she would rotate my legs by holding my feet up and then massage my temples. It was pure bliss. When my instructor talked about meditation with Deepak Chopra and davidji, I listened intently. I slowly began following davidji and started to attempt more frequent meditation sessions. I finally went to the Meditation Nest in Carlsbad for five glorious days with davidji and a group of like-minded souls. Hooked on getting in touch with the stillness and silence that rested within me, I looked forward to being in the "gap" between thoughts and finding the blissful state of pure joy that resides in my soul. davidji opened a whole new world to me. I am deeply grateful to him.

Overcoming challenges and conquering fears had been an enormous part of my life and story, and the inevitable change to conquer in the business was dealing with being older. I was confronted with the question: "Do I cave in, go gray, and accept the fact that I'm older and the work is just not that plentiful?" Women over fifty have a very small percentage of the work, and I didn't look like a grandma yet. On the advice of my agent, I bought a frightening gray wig to try to compete for the old lady stunt roles. At an audition at Disney Studios, my old friend Vince Deadrick, Jr. walked in, and I looked like a spinster school marm with this tight, curly, short-haired gray wig, wire-rimmed glasses, and a dowdy pink-flowered satin suit. I could barely look at myself in the mirror. When Vince saw me, he just about fell over laughing! I could hardly handle the embarrassment. It would have been different if I already had the job and then got made up to look like that.

But walking around in public, seeing my neighbors and old friends in that getup, was just too much to bear. I wasn't ready to assume that look on a regular basis no matter what the money was like. My enlightening moment was realizing that I would rather be cast as a cougar than a gray-haired grandma. In fact, right after that embarrassing moment, where I did not get the job, I got a job playing a cougar in the television show *Workaholics*, flirting with the lead character who was all of twenty-one years old. Hey, it was better than cutting my hair and turning gray any day of the week. I would continue to get cast frequently as a cougar, along with my Ferrari. I had the opportunity to work on the television show *Mistresses*, which was a blast, and

I showed up in front of a night club driving my Ferrari with a much younger guy. He was so cute and appreciative of his first Ferrari ride with a cougar!

I managed to stay in shape by kick boxing, dancing hip-hop, hiking, riding horses, and walking on the beach—along with a little golf thrown in there, too! My zest for life and attitude continued to be that of a young filly kicking her heels in the green verdant pasture. We all have obstacles to overcome and crosses to bear, especially as we age, but it's how we look at them that makes the difference. If we choose to embrace change and relish the transition periods, then the future will continue to look bright.

I've always been blessed to have my faith as my rock and guide in troubled times. Having God close by my side at all times has meant that I've never been alone. Feeling at peace, I deeply cherish my meditation times and working on my inner self. Listening to the surf, I learn the wisdom of the ages.

Today my real estate career with Coldwell Banker in Malibu greatly supplements my income. I'm also a member of the International President's Elite, a designation for top producers at Coldwell Banker. It's a challenge and joy to use my sharp negotiating skills and mathematical acumen to find the perfect homes for my wonderful clients and friends. My brand is Living the Dream Malibu, https://www.livingthedreammalibu.com, and I feel I am truly living the dream.

My heart will always lie in the television and film business that allowed my dreams to become a reality in so many wonderful ways. If I had to do it all over again, my only change would be to make better choices in marriage partners. Today I'm content with loving life and listening to the surf. So, I'll keep my long blond hair and million-dollar smile intact and enjoy the good life in Malibu, my heaven on earth.

In early 2016, I received a call from Doug Koban, a committee member for the Elmwood Park Centennial Parade that was to be held on June 12, 2016. He explained that my dear friend Annamarie Beilschmidt Witham suggested that I be invited to participate in the centennial parade as the Hollywood Stuntwoman, and everyone on the committee had wholeheartedly agreed. Doug also told me that he remembered me riding my horse at the football games when I was in high school! Extending the official invitation, Doug said that they would love for me to return to Elmwood Park and be in the parade, riding in a vintage convertible car. I was thrilled to be invited, but I told him that I needed to check my schedule and get back to him.

The more I thought about it, the cooler I thought it would be to honor the town I grew up in and pay tribute to my mom and dad who raised me there.

"I need to ride a horse in the parade," I decided, "I'm a stuntwoman!"

When I contacted Doug to tell him to count me in, I asked him if they had a permit for horses in the parade. He said they did because the Bergen County Mounted Police were going to be there. I proudly explained that I'd be riding a horse in the parade for sure. All I had to do was find one!

I googled "Parade Horses for Rent in New Jersey," and I found a Clydesdale farm in Long Valley, which was about an hour away from Elmwood Park. I called the Willow Grove Farm and talked to a sweet man named Winn. Explaining that I was a stuntwoman and an experienced horsewoman, I said that I needed to rent a Clydesdale for the upcoming parade.

Winn replied, "I have a gentle giant that you can ride."

When I asked him how we could ink the deal he said, "Your word is good enough for me."

True Jersey style! I liked him immediately.

The day before the parade, I flew to New Jersey and drove out to the farm with my brother. When I'd asked Doug if my brother could bring his vintage 1983 Boxer Ferrari, he said they would welcome him in the parade with a car like that. He was thrilled! Now we both could enjoy being in the parade.

When we met Winn at the rural farm, he showed us twenty gorgeous Clydesdales to choose from. I picked Kade, an enormous, 19.2 hand, seven-year-old, stunning Clydesdale with blue eyes. After climbing onto his huge frame with the help of a tall step ladder, we immediately were moving as one. I loved his thunderous stride and frisky spirit. Winn observed that I could handle the gentle giant, and we made a plan to meet at ten o'clock the next morning at Elmwood Park High School, the staging area for the parade.

Kade arrived right on time for the parade, looking gorgeous. His shining chestnut coat was glimmering in the morning sun, and his fetlocks were a brilliant bright white. He was feeling frisky and a bit nervous when I first mounted him because of all the distractions in the unfamiliar setting. Large floats with streamers flying sailed past us, and the bands tuning their instruments were making shrieking sounds. Kids were banging on drums and trumpets were blaring.

Patting Kade's neck, I spoke gently to him, "Easy big boy, settle down."

The Bergen County mounted police horses looked like miniatures compared to Kade. As we approached the start area of the parade, the excitement made butterflies churn in my stomach. I made small circles to keep Kade moving and to calm him down.

When I finally got the signal to go, there were two men carrying a banner that read, "Diane Peterson, Hollywood Stuntwoman."

I wore a red cowboy hat, red cowboy boots, and had a red satin sash with "Hollywood Stuntwoman" draped over my white cowgirl shirt.

Some of the people in the crowds were yelling, "Hi Diane, remember me? That's the biggest horse I've ever seen!"

I just kept smiling and waving and felt so blessed to be part of the centennial celebration of my hometown.

When we marched past my parents' house along the route, I know Dad and Mom were watching from above. I could hear my daddy say, "You do your daddy proud."

It was a glorious day and I felt I'd come full circle from riding a tiny pony in the parade when I was a child until now, on the mighty Clydesdale.

Life is good. God is great!

Overcome your fears and always follow your dreams. You will never regret it!

Epilogue

Since I finished this book, life has continued to unfold in the most wonderful ways. I traveled to Mexico with davidji and a group of seekers of the meditation practice. davidji's book, *Sacred Powers*, is a dynamic guide to help all on their path to enlightenment. Journeying the world with davidji is always a delight and a soul-opening experience. My trip to India with davidji was also unforgettable. While I was meditating under the Bodhi Tree, I was given a message, "To consider it all pure joy."

I also had the honor of being inducted into the Elmwood Park Athletic Hall of Fame at a banquet where I was presented with a gorgeous plaque for my achievements in equestrian and auto racing events. Surrounded by family and friends, I gave a heartfelt speech about growing up in Elmwood Park, New Jersey. I'm so very proud of this special honor and am confident my parents are beaming in heaven.

In November of 2018, I received a text from Callie Croughwell, stunt coordinator Charlie Croughwell's daughter, inquiring if I was available for work. Callie said that I would be a passenger on a capsizing boat with thirty-six stuntpeople aboard for the film *Laundromat*, starring Meryl Streep. I happily accepted the job, thrilled be working again for Charlie and looking forward to seeing many stuntpeople with whom I hadn't worked in years.

Two weeks before Thanksgiving, all hell broke loose in Malibu when wildfires blew through our community. Security guards were banging on my door at 8:30 a.m. telling me I had to evacuate my condo because the fire was approaching with lightning speed. I gathered a few clothes, a box of important papers, my stunt bag, and my precious Frenchie, Paco. My sweet boy Mack had passed away the year before. We jumped into the Ferrari and were faced with bumper-to-bumper traffic on Pacific Coast Highway, everyone making a frantic effort to outrun the fire. I could see threatening flames just over the nearby hill. I decided that if the fire got any closer, I would abandon the Ferrari, take Paco in my arms, and jump in the ocean. Slowly we inched away from the billowing clouds of smoke. Terrified, I was keenly aware that this wasn't a movie; it was the real deal. I made it safely to my Coldwell Banker office on Malibu Road.

While there was no power in the office, a handful of my colleagues were there supporting each other and trying to figure out what to do next. We watched in horror as the flames began consuming the hillsides. Just before dark, when it appeared that the winds were blowing the fire west, away from my condo, I decided to return home. It was extremely smoky, and a dark cloud hung over the condo complex like an ominous veil. At about eight o'clock in the evening, I walked to the upper parking lot and firefighters were talking to the handful of neighbors who remained. Because the entire city of Malibu was under mandatory evacuation, the firefighters assured us that they would be in the neighborhood in the event that the fire changed direction and returned to our domain. Even though it was a mandatory evacuation, a few of us stayed home.

Before I went to sleep, I devised a plan to gently toss Paco over the balcony from my first-floor unit to a bush below. Then I'd climb over the balcony, jump down, and run into the ocean with Paco if the fire licked at my door.

In the morning, the smoke was as thick as the smoke at a Texas barbeque. My head ached and my stomach was upset, but thank God, Paco and I were safe. Although there was no power and very little cell service, the worst was over for us. The few remaining residents formed a strong bond. We'd survived and helped one another.

Monday morning, I had to report to work on the movie in Lake Arrowhead. While the city was still under mandatory evacuation, I asked my very kind neighbor Steve to look after Paco. It was difficult to leave while fires still burned in Malibu. And I knew I'd not be able to return until the evacuation order was lifted.

Paco had plenty of food, so I kissed my little buddy goodbye.

I drove to the Ontario airport where the production had instructed us to leave our cars. I'd taken the Ferrari just in case the fire returned. And Steve promised to take Paco if he had to evacuate. Boarding the shuttle for the hour-plus drive to Lake Arrowhead, I loved seeing some of my old stunt buddies, especially George Fisher. When we arrived at Lake Arrowhead, we were escorted to a large holding area and met by the hair department. They decided that I needed a brownish-gray wig to accentuate my new look as a retired traveler from Minnesota. It was windy and blisteringly cold as we boarded the small boat, *The Ethan Allen*. The film was the true story of the overloaded *Ethan Allen* that capsized in 2005 on Lake George in New York, where twenty passengers drowned. The boat owners thought they had insurance, but it was a bogus offshore company that was laundering money. After getting set with wardrobe, we were taken to a funky motel to spend the night.

Early the next morning, grateful we didn't have to plunge into the freezing cold waters of Lake Arrowhead, we began shooting the exterior shots of us boarding the boat and going for a joyride. The tank at Universal would be used for the capsizing boat.

A few days later, we had a rehearsal day at Universal. Arriving at the tank called Falls Lake in the back lot at Universal, I saw that the *Ethan Allen* was on a rotisserie-type mechanism whereby it could fully capsize. Then a crane with a thick cable attached to the boat would upright it.

The plan was that the boat would capsize on the port side, and that's where I was placed. George Fisher was on my left and Tommy Rosales was on my right. As we discussed the timing and our direction once the boat began to take on water, we observed the boast capsizing at different speeds while we were standing on dry land.

Early the next morning, I arrived at Universal and drove past the haunted castle as thick fog was rising. It was so cool! I got dressed in my wet suit for rehearsal and had my hair pinned down in preparation for the wig. Because the director, Steven Soderbergh, wanted to rehearse with only wet suits and no wigs, I showed up with a stocking cap on.

We first did the roll of the boat at half speed. Picking my spot, I pushed off the railing as the boat flipped over. My adrenaline was pumping, and I was loving it. Although it all went well, I knew that it was only half speed and things would happen much quicker. During the second rehearsal, at three quarter speed, I had to hustle to get out of the boat in order to allow time for

George and Tommy to exit. Checking in with each other after we surfaced, we all felt good about going full speed ahead.

The full-speed rehearsal happened fast! As soon as I realized the boat was filling with water, I was gone in a shot. My heart was beating like hummingbird wings. Now we were finally ready to get wigged and dressed for the filming.

The wig was secured to my head like a bird's nest to a tree. The last thing we wanted was a wig floating in the shot! I dressed in wardrobe's heavy winter sweater and khaki pants for the shot and kept my wet suit on for buoyancy. When we boarded the boat, I felt that amazing, familiar adrenaline rush pulsating through my body. Grateful that my longing for this feeling was being fed, I breathed in deeply and savored the moment. I joked with George that I had a "sinking feeling," and we laughed and hugged. As the director counted down to rolling and action, we were ready.

The boat flipped quickly, as I anticipated, and I dove under and away from the boat. After getting kicked in the shin by someone, I surfaced, looked for George, and spotted him. Scanning for Tommy, I smiled when he gave me a thumbs-up. It felt so wonderful to be back in action, doing what I loved to do. Of course, we needed to do several more takes with different camera angles. Each time was a joy, filling a special place in my heart and soul of doing what I do best: stunts!

Dreams do come true if you follow them and believe in yourself.

Acknowledgments

There are so many wonderful friends who helped me on my journey, and I thank you all with deep gratitude. I will start by thanking my dear sweet mom and dad who gave me the core strength to know that I could do everything and anything I put my mind to. Many thanks to my wonderful brother, John, who always was and still is the most amazing brother anyone could ever ask for. My best friend, Babe Watts, a better friend one could never find. Much love. Many thanks to Carolyn Hunter for suggesting that I write this book. Her friendship and encouragement helped me so very much. Special thanks to my dear friends Reverend J. Patrick Kelly, Annamarie Beilschmidt Witham, Dana Dru Evenson Taavon, Mary Peters, Margot Strong, Lorraine Schannon, Joanie Caggiano, Cristina Roggero, Maggie Luckerath, and Emily Mateu. Gratitude to Monona Wali, my memoir writing teacher, who taught me that there is more to the book than just action sequences. William Gladstone, Tara Gladstone, and Josh Freel, thank you for believing in my book and getting it published. Margot Starbuck, thank you for editing my book. To davidji, my guru, your guidance has blessed my life, namaste. Alex Stevens, rest in peace, you gave me my first break. Many thanks to all the stunt coordinators who trusted me to get the job done. Most of all, I thank God for my life and giving me the courage to overcome my fears and follow my dreams.